Get Over It!
How to Bounce Back after Hitting Rock Bottom for Teens

Adair f. White-johnson, Ph.D.

Published by

Johnson Tribe Publishing, LLC

Atlanta, GA

Copyright © 2013 by Adair f. White-johnson, Ph.D.

All rights reserved, including the express right to reproduce this book or portions thereof in any form whatsoever whether now known or hereinafter developed. For information address Johnson Tribe Publishing, P.O. Box 1587 Powder Springs, Georgia 30127.

Johnson Tribe Publishing materials may be purchased for education, business, or promotional use. Author is also available for speaking engagements. For information please contact us at (888) 400-7302, email us at johnsontribepublishing@gmail.com or visit us at www.johnsontribepublishing.com

The following story is inspired by actual events. However, the names have been changed to protect the privacy of those involved.

Manufactured in the United States of America

10 9 8 7 6 5 4 3 2 1

FIRST EDITION – July 2013

Creative Direction: Adair F. White-johnson, Ph.D.

Edited by: Amanda J. Perkins, Soulful Storytellers, Inc.

Graphic Design: Stacey Bowers, August Pride, LLC

Book Design: Adair F. White-Johnson, Ph.D.

Library of Congress Catalog Card Number:

ISBN-13: 978-0989673303
ISBN-10: 0989673308

USA $12.95

Canada $15.50

DEDICATION

TO THE DAUGHTER WHO TAUGHT ME HOW TO LOVE A TEENAGER...ANYWAY.

SUSAN B. RIGGINS-JOHNSON

2/28/14

Nicki,

Thank You Sooo Much for Your Support!!

Adam

CONTENTS

	Introduction	i
Part I	G: Getting over yourself	1
Part II	O: Overcoming Your Odds	5
Part III	H: Hesitancy, Heart, Honesty, Hustling, Healthy Balance	11
Part IV	A: Anger, Artillery	23
Part V	R: Remembrance, Resilience, Restoration, Renewal, Righteousness	38
Part VI	D: Dreams, Depth, Destiny	54
Part VII	Ways your parents can help you to *Get Over It!*	61
Part VIII	Just "plain ol' stuff" *to Get Over It!*	76
Part IX	Twelve Tricks to *Get Over It!*	92
Part X	What you need to *Get Over It!*	94
	Conclusion	99

INTRODUCTION

I am writing this "book" because for many years I have constantly been asked "how do you do it all?" "How do you manage your life so it flows so easily?" At first, I was a little taken aback by these questions because I didn't think that my life was easy and it never had been easy. I knew what I had gone through to become the woman that I am but I also knew that folks were only looking at the finished product and really didn't know the story behind the actual process. They didn't know how I "got here." They were not aware of my personal value and belief system, the heartache and the sacrifices I've endured nor did they know about the abundance of blessings that I received. All they wanted to know was "how do you do it?" I thought that I lived my life like many others but after receiving so many inquiries about how I manage life, how "I do it," I began to think that perhaps there was more to my story than I ever realized. People wanted to know my formula for success…I looked at it as just my unique approach to my life…Happiness is my ultimate goal so I have crafted a system that works for me as long as I work for it…I am dedicated to everything that I do and I commit only to excellence…I take my mistakes as lessons learned and I only stumble softly from them. I work hard to "go hard" and this is what this book is all about.

It was during my teenage years that I think my greatest metamorphosis occurred. I learned what my strengths and weaknesses were, what I really believed in and how to create plans to make my dreams come true. These years were significant in my intellectual, social, emotional and spiritual growth because it was the time that I experienced the most "change" in my life. I learned how to "just be me" and I learned how to become that woman that I was destined to be. It was also a scary and confusing time that I knew would impact the rest of my life but somehow I also believed that everything would be alright…once I figured it out. I absorbed a lot during that time…I had good and bad relationships with my family, friends, teachers and boyfriends that really became the blueprints of what my relationships look like today. It was definitely a time of change for me so I understand what you are going through at this moment. My grades sucked and I knew that I really wasn't "dumb" but felt like everything else was getting in the way of my academic success. School was just not the priority although I knew it was supposed to be at that moment in time and I was angry because I wanted a better life for myself but wasn't sure how to make that happen.

Although I have never walked a mile in your shoes I do understand what it feels like to walk anywhere and sometimes walk alone. This book focuses on what I did and what I know should be done to give your walks direction...to help you to *Get Over It!*, get through it and keep it moving.

This book provides a glimpse into my world...the things that I do daily that keep me on the right side of life. It explains the things that I do to "*Get Over It!*" Am I perfect? NOT! But am I a fighter? YES I am! With every inhaled breath that I breathe and to the core of my soul I fight for my sanity, blessings and existence daily. These are the skills that have worked for me over the years and I strongly believe that if you give life the best that you have then these can work for you too! "*Getting Over It*" is not just doing things, because it is a mindset. It is about believing that you can "get over it" despite life's circumstances, socioeconomic status, race, class and perhaps even gender. And when life is rough and you fall down, you do it softly and you get right back up again. It's mind over matter, as much as you mind is as much as it matters and if you don't mind, then it shouldn't matter...

I have created an acronym that describes the strategies I've used in my lifetime to "*Get Over*" things, situations and people. This acronym, "Go Hard" will be the focus of this book and the foundation you can use to make positive changes in your life. The book is divided into several parts with six sections aligned with the "Go Hard" philosophy. The remaining sections share strategies and techniques to assist you in your goal to *"Get Over It!"*

Throughout this book I have included poetry that I have written over the years that I believe speak volumes about my life and provide more insight about my thought process and experiences. These poems were written throughout my lifetime but I am including them in the sections of the book where I think they are most applicable. Remember, these are *my* words that reflect *my* feelings about *my* life and me *Going Hard*…The poem below reflects my thoughts about living in my skin knowing that I often think about the world differently than many others but also embracing that as a strength…Acknowledging that it can be problematic for others though….

<u>A Square World</u>

Living as a square in a circular world can be a challenging life.

Your edges may be too sharp and your corners too perpendicular for a round mind. As a square you can embrace the ability to move your thoughts in different directions…and still land right side up.

You love your diversified positions…Right angle today but perhaps just a vertical line tomorrow.

I am a complex square with a diverse personality and fascinating dimensions to my behavior.

And sometimes circles just don't understand.

Circles begin and end in the same place while squares can opt to remain in one position or go to the other side.

Squares can be divided to reflect the measurements of the soul.

But I wonder how circles bend to see the inside of their cores….Hmmmm

The challenge becomes when a circle is in a perceived position of power and attempts to redesign the

square to fit within their circle…What happens then?

Does the square become an obtuse angle? Or perhaps a right angle?

Or, does the square simply retreat into its four corners and wait for the circle to just bounce away?

PART I
G= GETTING OVER YOURSELF TO *GET OVER IT!*

This is the first task to *Go Hard*. We often spend a ridiculous amount of time complaining about things that have happened in our past that we simply won't let go and it impacts how we approach our future choices. We think and talk about what "shoulda, coulda, woulda been" but the fact is that it "simply wasn't." Letting go and healing ourselves is one of the most challenging tasks that we can conquer but you have to do this to get over yourself. If you don't then you become so self-absorbed and wallowing in your pain that you can't truly feel for others because what you feel for them will be based upon what you feel for yourself at any given moment.

For example, I know a young woman who lost both parents at a young age. As she grew up her life took various twists and turns and ultimately she began to make poor choices that impacted her adult life. You see this young girl never allowed herself to heal and release the emotions that she felt about both parents suddenly dying…issues of abandonment. She continuously put Band-Aids on gunshot wounds but never went in and did the surgery on her wounds so ultimately her heart and soul were infected and she cannot get over her hurt, pain and "herself." All issues in her life have been swallowed up in her pit of despair and never directly cleansed. She can't get over herself because she thinks that she cannot reach her true self any longer. Her life is robust with actions and reactions that are based upon lies, deceit and impulsivity. She cannot be true to anyone or her own life because she hasn't been true to herself and still continues to lie to herself. You know you got it bad when you lie to yourself and then you start believing your own lies because you think the truth is too difficult to manage. You begin to build walls around your heart and your soul and live in somewhat of a fantasy world that life is good. Are you guilty of doing this? How can you get over hurt and pain and tragic life events if you cannot deal with them directly?

You see, getting over yourself means that you have to be able to get through to yourself…clean out your internal emotional closet and just let stuff go. Make room for the good life and good times. Don't borrow worries. Getting over yourself means not wallowing in self-pity over the things that happened in your past…regardless of whether it was your fault or not…letting it go gives you the power to get over it. Everybody has problems and you shouldn't feel special because you know that you have problems too…you're not…At least you're not special for that reason. Get over yourself believing that your issues make you special and therefore you don't have to try to improve your state of mind and your state of being…you can't love hard and be hard if you can't get over yourself hard first.

I know. I understand and I get it. My life did not begin as it is now…there was an abundance of hurt and pain. I was twelve the first time I tried to commit suicide. It was right after I had been beaten with belts and broomsticks by Ma (my mother) and Mr. James (her boyfriend) in the back storage room of the liquor store they owned and operated. Why was I beaten? Because I went to the library on St. Marks and Nostrand Avenues with my friends Gale and Kaitlyn but Ma didn't believe me…she thought I was lying and sneaking around with boys. I didn't even know how to sneak around at that point! So she beat me and tried to beat me some more in hopes of getting a confession out of me. And then she had Mr. James come in and beat me…I had lumps on my legs from the broomsticks and jumping over the boxes in the storage room and falling to the floor. This time it felt like it was "one beating too many." When I was finally released and allowed to go home, I just wanted to be "free." I needed to feel numb because it was one thing to be beaten when you are dead wrong but quite another to receive such a brutal beating when you have done *nothing* wrong. I knew that if I could go to live in a "better place" then God would take care of me.

That afternoon I took 13 Tylenol pills along with a couple of drinks from Ma's vodka bottle that she kept hidden under the cushion of the couch that she slept on. I remember falling asleep on that couch shortly after taking the pills but awakening to the sound of the phone ringing persistently. It was one of those old rotary phones and it was in the hallway of the apartment so we kept the ringer up loud so we could hear it from all rooms.

Rinngggggg....rinnnggggg...rinnnggggg....the shrilling sound was pulsating in my ears and I was awakened...I got up to answer the phone and it was Ma and then I realized "Dang, I am still alive."

During this time in my life I barely existed. I got up and I functioned...and functioned with a smile on my face so no one could see the pain within. I knew it didn't feel right but these were my own demons and no one else had to know about them... I still wear masks to this very day to *Go Hard*. I keep many of my feelings inside...never wearing them on my shoulders and not wanting to be the poster child for pain. It's not that I don't deal with my feelings I just find it unnecessary to wear those feelings on my shoulders with folks who really don't care and I learned how to "play the game." Smiling on the outside but I may be trembling with fear and anguish on the inside. A friend of mine once described me as a "dichotomous duplicity." He explained that it's almost like I have a dual personality...you may know one side of me and know that side for many years but there is another side that if you really paid attention you may get a glimpse of it. This is the side of me that only the selected people in my square are allowed to see. Not dwelling on tragedy, hurt and pain of the past allows me to control my feelings, to get over me and to *Go Hard*. If I were to spend my time and energy focusing on all of the negative things and negative people in my life then chances are that I would become a negative person. Negative people CANNOT "*Go Hard*" because they spend too much time going negative. So if you stumble over yourself and others around you then you have to remember to get up and get over yourself so you can *Go Hard!*

What are the things that can stagger your ability to Go Hard?

PART II

O= OVERCOMING YOUR ODDS TO *GET OVER IT!*

This is another facet to *"Go Hard."* This step focuses on not embracing the future that statistics has presented to you but instead using your own life experiences as the threshold to make improvements. This is the point where you use where YOU have come from to determine where it is that you will go in the future. Yes, we all know that there are academic achievement gaps between Caucasians and African Americans and Hispanics. We know that there are still salary differences between males and females and we know that in contemporary society poverty still begets poverty. BUT, is that YOUR story? Is that where you come from?

My example here is my own life story…statistically speaking I should not have graduated high school at sixteen years old, completed college within 3 ½ years, received my master's degree a year later and earn a doctoral degree within several years of receiving my Certificate of Advanced Studies. Since I grew up in economic poverty on the streets of Brooklyn it was assumed that I grew up in intellectual poverty as well. Statistics showed that I could have been one of the approximately 18.4% of African American students who dropped out of high school in 1982…[i] That's because I was raised in a single-parent household living below the poverty line with an alcoholic, abusive mother and I shouldn't have "made it." The statistical odds were against me but I refused to let those odds determine my fate. I believed that there were already enough odds stacked up against me from my own family history and background. Instead, I looked at my life experiences and began to rank my new experiences against those.

When we lived on St. Marks Ave in Brooklyn we were probably the poorest family on the block…at least it felt like it…We lived among filth because my grandmother (Mom Belk) was elderly and physically limited and my mother simply ignored the dirt. So we lived in a two bedroom apartment with the roaches and mice. When you walked into the kitchen at night you would have to stomp on the kitchen floor to scare the mice and make the roaches scatter. You couldn't leave any food on the counter because the mice would come out and eat the food. In fact, that's how I learned that mice loved chocolate! I brought home a box of chocolate bars from school to sell as a part of a fundraiser and I left the box on the counter. The next morning I discovered the mice had eaten through the box, the paper and the foil that covered the chocolate bars. The entire $30 box was ruined and I was too embarrassed to explain to my teacher what happened to the chocolate bars so the $30 debt remained on my record until I was scheduled to graduate four years later and my uncle paid the fee so I could receive my high school diploma.

The heat never worked right either and it was never warm enough in the apartment. I remember Mom Belk used to turn the oven on and close the back room (dining room) door so we could have heat back there. We would pile up in that back room to stay warm and we were afraid to get up to go to the bathroom in the middle of the night because you knew that your butt would get cold so you couldn't pull your underwear all the way down…you squatted real fast and got out of there because there was no heat. You could actually see your breath when you blew outward; it was that cold in the apartment. I used to sit on the radiators throughout the day while in junior high school because I thought that if I saved enough heat in my body from school then somehow I would be warmer at home.

I didn't have a bed…I slept on the floor with Mom Belk…she made pallets and we used to snuggle up right next to each other to be warm. I remember her having a tapestry with a picture of Jesus on it that belonged on the wall which she took down because it was sooooo heavy and she knew it would keep us warm. She said that we would always be protected because it was a tapestry of Jesus and he covered us nightly. Mom Belk and I slept under that tapestry on the floor for many years…just to keep warm and be protected by Jesus. And that's when I began to just think…and dream some more about how I could overcome my own odds. How could I rise up and fly away to find my own stars amid the pitch black night sky?

What did I need to do to fulfill my own dreams and beat those statistics that had spoken volumes for my so-called silenced future? What could I do to stumble through this pain and how could I "go hard" to ease the throbbing that I felt inside of me so that I could feel warm, safe and protected? I knew that a change had to be in the forecast for me and it had to be a positive change because I felt that all the negative things that could have happened to me had already occurred. I really felt that there was no place for me to go but "up" because I had lived in rock bottom for so long already. Little did I know how dramatic the change was going to be in my life and I didn't know how young I was going to be when I learned how to stumble softly and overcome my own odds.

When my mom died of alcoholism at the age of 37 and I was only 14, I figured that there wasn't anything worse that could happen to me from that point on. I convinced myself that the "hole" in my heart was so deep that no one else in the world would be allowed to hurt me that way. I knew that if I could "get over" my mom's death, then there wouldn't be any separation or hurt that I couldn't get over for the rest of my life so I used that pain as the armored truck to combat future suffrage.

I was failing in school at the time of her death and we lived in a roach infested tenement in Brooklyn without heat and hot water but I also knew that I had to get over myself and overcome my own odds to become a future success. I used my own life experience as my motivation and inspiration because I knew the emotional and psychological state of mind that I was left in after Ma died. Yes, I was a victim of physical, emotional, psychological and sexual abuse under her watch but she was still *my* mother and I loved her. I actually felt lost without her… I had to become that foot soldier emerging from those trenches of disparity to defy these odds…it didn't matter what statistics noted because those numbers didn't live with me daily…heartache, loneliness, emptiness, sorrow and shame had taken residence in my life and it didn't feel good. I knew that I wasn't happy and set forth to move out of that depressive state…against my own odds.

If you are going hard, then you have to overcome your own odds…get over what you have "been through." We have all "been through" stuff in our lives but that doesn't give us a "pass" to continue allowing abuse, neglect and mis-education to set up permanent residence in our lives…Know YOUR story and overcome the odds in YOUR life to push through the pain…*Get Over It!* get through it and keep it moving to *"Go Hard."*

So how do you do this?

1. *Be honest with yourself. Who are you really?* Take a few minutes weekly and look into that mirror. Stare at yourself and what do you see? Do you know that person? Or, is it simply a reflection of a person who no longer exists or never really was?

2. *Answer the tough questions that you ask yourself.* We spend so much time asking ourselves and God "Why?" and "Why did this have to happen to me?" Or, "What did I do to deserve

this?" Well, start to answer your own questions and if you are honest with yourself you will see that God has placed the answers in front of you all the while…you just have to want to see the truth.

3. *Push through the pain and find your inner peace.* Yes, it hurts! That's what pain does…it hurts! If you know this, then don't allow yourself to continuously sit through it! Would you leave your hand sitting in a fire? Probably not. So why would allow your heart and soul to drown in a pool of pain? Work through your issues in the best manner for you…Talking to positive people can be a start…whomever is in your life that can actually help you…a counselor, "sistagurlfriend", "bra-man" or family member. Find your "person" and let them help you…if they "really" love you then they don't want to see you living in pain so they will be there for you! And know that it is perfectly fine to ask to see a professional counselor. Sometimes sharing your thoughts and your feelings with someone who is removed from the situation can be quite helpful. The bottom line is that you should begin to reject behavior that denies the truth and answer those tough questions then you can begin to push through that pain to find that inner peace.

4. *Don't borrow worries.* As humans we can definitely find some problems to worry about! If they are not our own problems then we try to be helpful to assist someone else to solve their problems. Now I'm not saying we can't be helpful because Lord knows that is one of my greatest strengths but also one of my greatest weaknesses. What I am saying though is that in order to overcome your odds you can no longer worry about everything that goes on around you. You have to think of ways to get over that hump; those things that cause you

pain. You will need to focus on your own issues and you shouldn't have time to create more problems. Don't fill your lunchbox with items that you will not eat just because the food looked good. All that will happen when you do that is, you make your lunch bag heavy, the food is wasted or you just bring it right back home. You don't want to do that with the odds stacked against you. You don't want additional worries (excess "baggage") to weigh you down, you don't want to waste valuable time on things that really don't matter in your life and you definitely don't want to bring worries back home with you. So, to defy the odds of your own life, don't borrow those worries. There is an old negro spiritual that says "I don't worry about tomorrow, I just live day to day, I don't borrow from the sunshine…" That's what "don't borrow worries" is all about.

Defining and overcoming your own odds is an important step in recognizing the issues or problems which prohibit you from *Getting Over It!* If you know what the stumbling blocks are then you can move forward before those blocks are stacked higher against you and it becomes impossible to *Get Over It!*

PART III

H= HESITANCY, HEART, HONESTY, HUSTLING, HEALTHY BALANCE TO *GET OVER IT!*

Hesitancy:

Wow...what does all of that mean and how do I incorporate it in my life to *Go Hard*? Well, I really think that sometimes we do need to slow down and not act impulsively...I really take pride in my ability to critically think and analyze situations before taking action. When you hesitate it allows you to double check yourself and rethink what you are going to do. Yes, it can be frustrating for others but sometimes you just have to put yourself first and step back to ponder the situation. In my life I have been hesitant to do a lot of things because of fear of stumbling but I have taken great pride in living in my "square" even if the world around me has been a circle.

I have always been hesitant in my relationships with others. I have created an "inner square" of significant people in my life and I am extremely hesitant in letting others into this square. Although there is not a specific protocol that one has to follow to be a part of my world there are qualities and traits that I look for in people that would allow me to welcome them in. Positive outlooks in life, spirituality, dreamers and simply "good people" are the basic characteristics that I look for. Now, that's not to say that I don't associate myself with folks with problems...I do. But if you are a negative person as a result of your problems and experiences and you want the world to be negative along with you then I can't be around you...The old saying "misery loves company" has been true for soooo many folks that I meet who actually try to send out invitations to join them in their miserable lives! Those are the people who are not invited to MY island; my square! So yes, I am hesitant in my relationship with others and I am hesitant in trusting others. Based upon the lessons learned about stumbling softly, getting over myself and overcoming my own odds I recognize the previous mistakes made in my relationships with others and I choose not to repeat the same mistakes. I take a lesson away from every significant relationship that I have been a part of throughout my life. By doing this I am able to assess what aspects of relationships are healthy versus the toxic elements of unhealthy relationships. Knowing the toxins definitely allows me the ability to choose the folks in my world and hesitate to allow those who "hate on me" into my life.

Sometimes you should just sit back and think about "stuff" and hesitate to do "stuff" to allow yourself to make effective choices. Be hesitant about who you let in your world because some folks will try to destroy what you have…

Heart:

As much as I love to use my brains to help me think through situations I find that I can also make good choices and *Go Hard* when I use my *Heart* because that elicits raw emotions.

I already know that a double vision (heart and mind) is needed to coherently feel and using my heart allows me to "use my gut" and follow my instincts…sometimes those speak volumes themselves. It is a wonderful way of knowing…intuition. It can be used to guide you in those tough relationships with others and can help you determine what makes you feel good. When you listen to your heart everything else will follow. When you have a heart you will *Go Hard* and give everything that you have to ensure excellence. Because no one likes to be heartbroken you will fight from the depths of your soul to protect your heart so imagine if you put your heart into the important things or those things that matter in your life? You will work harder just to get harder and you will fight harder for your happiness and sanity. This is how you will *Get Over It!* For me, I always use my heart first when it comes to my children and then I pull my mind into situations.

As a mother of 4 biological boys and an adopted daughter I find that motherhood has been a great strength, weakness and challenge in my life. Each child is very different with a variety of needs and I have become a chameleon while raising them. My second son is Autistic...he has Asperger's Syndrome and since his differences became clear when he was two years old I have protected him by using my heart and gut first, then rely on my intelligence (mind) second. When sitting in his planning meetings at his school, I listen carefully to the suggested plan of action and I use my "heart gauge" to measure my feelings as to whether he is being treated fairly and "right." If what the school faculty says "feels right" then I allow my brain power to analyze, synthesize and evaluate the information for the development of an educational plan that will maximize his potential. I also know that over the years more people have learned *more* from him than he could ever learn from them. They have learned compassion, understanding, patience, dedication and acceptance from this boy...all through their interactions with him. My heart allows me to see this gift in my child but also to protect him from anyone who appears to challenge his very existence.

Another example is my relationship with my adopted daughter and the choices she periodically makes. My heart allows me to love her "as is" because I know who she is under the crafted persona. I know she is a "good" person who has made poor choices. My heart reminds me that it is not my place to judge the decisions that she made just because they do not fit into the square that I have built around my life. But my mind doesn't allow me to let her infuse *my* life in some parts of *her* life story.

I remember when I had to *Go Hard* with her as we took a weekend trip for fun. It was an awesome weekend until it was time to leave. She split her time between me, my sorority sister and other friends whom she met there. We decided on a time to leave to get on the road for the eight hour drive and it was inferred that I would be the designated driver. I was fine with that and agreed to leave at a designated time. When she didn't show up at the agreed upon time and after calling and texting her multiple times I made the decision to get on the road and drive myself back to Atlanta. Yes, I knew it was 10:45pm and I would drive all night but I needed to be back in ATL by 10am and this was the only way to make that happen. My heart told me to wait for my daughter, to understand her conflict, empathize with her psychological state of mind and to be more patient. My heart allowed me to *Go Hard* and not pass judgment on the choices she made that weekend…to love and accept her for who she is anyway but my mind was in control at that point and I had to *Go Hard*. I got in my car and drove myself 470 miles overnight to my final destination…All alone. As tough as it was for me emotionally sometimes you just do what you have to do…you just have to *Go Hard* to *Get Over It!* and you do this with heart and mind.

Going Hard with heart also allows you to give to others from a good place. I know that I absolutely love giving and doing for others just because I can. Christmas 2010 was perhaps one of the most heart-filled moments of giving for me. I used my heart to help a friend and my actions ended helping more than just my friends and since what comes around, goes around I ended up helping myself by my actions.

My girlfriend Cierra and I have been friends for about 18 years and we both have 4 boys but two of our boys are the same age. Najja and Mason grew up playing football and attending primary school together. Cierra and I discovered that we were kindred spirits by the time the boys were only 3 years old. We became good friends and that friendship remained through her divorce, "re-dating" phase and subsequent marriage to her new husband when she moved to another county and were unable to see each as often. We still remained in contact over the years…often only speaking on the phone every couple of months but the conversations always resumed where we left off. Najja and Mason were still playing football and we would see one another at the high school football games. Both boys were talented and were going to continue to play college football. In fact, Mason had received a full athletic scholarship to attend college.

Cierra and Mason were scheduled to come to Najja's high school graduation party when the boys were seniors but there was a schedule conflict. The following weekend was Mason's graduation but he never made it because he suffered a life-threatening spinal injury from a swimming pool accident the night before his graduation. Everyone was devastated and in shock --- Mason was now paralyzed from the neck down.

In the three years since the accident Cierra and Mason world changed because he went from being a basketball/football star to a wheelchair bound young man without the use of his limbs…he only had the ability to move his head and speak. As you can probably imagine this took a financial toll on the family (beyond the psychological and emotional) and Cierra took it day by day to make it work. Remember when I said she and I were kindred spirits? Well this was evident in her daily fight to ensure that her family was taken care of and that Mason had the best care. During the time I felt helpless, I didn't know what I could do to help my friend because this situation seemed to be beyond my reach. I knew that I was still a good friend serving as a part of her emotional support system but I knew she needed more financial help. I decided to write a letter explaining her needs to the local radio station that was sponsoring a contest at the time. They were soliciting letters from families and friends of people who were in need of specific things for Christmas. In other words they were granting Christmas wishes. I wrote a letter from my heart and explained to them what Cierra and Mason needed to make a difference in their lives and they actually selected my letter and granted my Christmas wish for them. They even gave them "extra stuff" because they empathized with the turmoil that Cierra, Mason and their family still experienced. You see, I let my *Heart* work for me when I wrote that letter and with the talent that God gave me of expressing my feelings via the written word I was able to make a positive difference in Cierra's life and help her. Thousands of people heard us on the radio show that morning and many others reached out to help Cierra and family. Various folks contacted me to thank me for writing the letter to the station and sharing Cierra's story. My letter had touched the hearts of many and changed the life of others. The heart allows you to do this and when you embrace this you can *Get Over It!* Use your heart to *Go Hard* sometimes because you can only be stronger because of it.

Honesty:

Honesty is another facet of the "H" in *Go Hard*. Hmmmm....you know that you struggle with honesty if you begin to believe the lies that you tell yourself. When you begin to think that fantasy life that you are living is reality to you. If you are untrue to yourself then chances are that you are untrue to others around you. I think that if you struggle to look in the mirror to see who is really staring back at you then you are probably unlikely to share with others who that person really is inside of you. I find that folks who cannot accept certain things about themselves and choose not to make changes to those negative things are the same folk who will lie to themselves...their entire lives becomes lies and thus they live a lie daily...For me, I think that is a whole lot of work! I want to expend my energy doing things that make me feel good about myself, make my family proud of me and make me want to look into the mirror. That's what I strive to do daily and that's what keeps me going on a daily basis. Is it scary at times? Yes. I remember many moments when I would look in the mirror and wasn't sure of the person who was staring back at me...it just felt like the reflection of a person that never really was. When I was fifteen years old I wrote this short poem that really captured this feeling:

Empty Reflections

Sometimes when I look in the mirror and there isn't anyone looking back at me,

Just an empty reflection of a person that never really was. Just a shadow of many dreams that have gone unfulfilled. No hopes, desires or needs that have been accomplished.

Oh, how I stare into those glaring eyes – hoping to get a glimpse of the soul inside

But instead, all that I see…

Is that empty reflection staring back at me.

I used this poem over the years as my own inspiration to get beyond that empty reflection because I knew how alone and hurt that I often felt. I used it as insight when I felt myself stumbling backwards. When I would read it I would force myself to look in that mirror again and stare into my own eyes to see if I could actually find where the hurt and pain lay. The only way that I could move away from that empty reflection was to be true to myself...honest with who I am, what I do and what I stand for. I figured that if I could face my own reflection without any shame, guilt, or remorse then I could face the world with strength and perseverance. Is this easy? No. But as Michael Jackson wrote in his song you must first "start with the man in the mirror." Be honest with yourself to improve yourself and to make your life a positive reality instead of a frustrating fantasy. Find that mirror and use those eyes to stare into your soul. You can't *Get Over It! and Go Hard* if you are not honest with yourself.

Who do you see when you look into the mirror?

Hustling:

Now I know this may sound "ghetto" but I think it's important that you always have a "hustle." Having a hustle implies that you always have something going on, that you are making "moves" that lead toward change. In my life I have attempted to keep my "hustles" positive. I align my hustles with my dreams…when I finish one, I get another so I never stop hustling and I never stop dreaming. This is how you "keep it moving" and accomplish your goals.

I think I started hustling around the age of eight years old when I realized that in order to get some of the things that I wanted or needed I would have to create a plan. Remember, living with my mom was financially tough so anything "extra" had to be earned. I began by babysitting some of the kids of my mom's friends and running errands to the corner store for the elderly in my building. "Uncle Freddy" and "Uncle Val" had limited mobility so they needed someone to run to the store for them. Sometimes I would write out the price labels, lick them and then stick them on the back of the liquor bottles for my mom in the liquor store where she worked and she would pay me a few dollars for the job. I did all of this at such a young age because I knew that I would have to "make" things happen in my life and not just sit around and "let" things happen. Those things I could control, I tried to…Hustling was a part of ensuring a viable future for myself.

I've always had quite a few hustles going on…Years ago I had a colleague, Careena, whom I would laugh and share our hustles because we had a similar mindset regarding hustling. She and I would actually sit and make lists of what we could do to best utilize our skills. We even created a business together that we hustled for a couple of years while still working full-time and part-time elsewhere. I've worked in McDonald's while selling polo shirts to friends served as an afterschool counselor while working full-time as a high school counselor but also playing receptionist at a modeling agency at the same time. I've sold winter coats and various brand-name handbags over the years and I'm still a Mary Kay consultant! I've worked two full-time jobs at the same time while teaching online at another university simultaneously. I actually cannot remember a time when I didn't have at least 2 jobs and at least one hustle going on. I can't say that it's all about the money either. For me, in many instances I really feel self-fulfilled...I feel empowered and I feel worthy. I pick and choose my hustles because I know that my heart and soul will be invested in it so I have to feel aligned to it. Money can buy many things but I don't believe that it can buy self-fulfillment. My hustling is also used philanthropically as well.

Over the past six years I have raised over $15,000 for the Lupus Foundation of Georgia via my participation in the annual Lupus Walk. Each year I set a personal goal for the fundraising effort and then I "get my hustle on" to achieve my goal. I haven't missed a goal yet! My hustling skills extend beyond working to just make money...they extend to hustling to just make a difference.

Having the skills and the mindset of a hustler forces you to keep it moving and you just never, ever give up. If one dream doesn't work out you move on to the next one. When one hustle is up you create a new one. Hustling requires setting a goal and creating a plan to achieve that goal. It demands that you commit to excellence and that you know the purpose of the hustle and you never lose sight of this purpose. I am fortunate that I come from a family of hustlers...I come from a family who always worked, always were involved in "something." Mom Belk used to say "it's not *what* you do to work, it is *how* you do it at work" and although she didn't embrace illegal professions she wanted me to know that I just needed pride in whatever I did because that's what I would be remembered for. So, any hustle that I am involved in I hustle with pride, dignity, grace, perseverance, motivation, dedication and with heart….Yes, you gotta have a hustle to move forward in this world and you definitely need a hustle to *Go Hard!*

What's your hustle?

Healthy Balance:

Finally, to enjoy and respect your life I think you need to find that "healthy balance" between all things that are important to you. This requires deleting unimportant facets of your life and lifestyle. Sometimes there is simply just too much to accomplish in one day and if you have all of the "good stuff" entangled with the "negative stuff" then how will you successfully make it through the day? I used to tell my oldest son all the time that it wasn't necessary to be the best at *everything* every time…what was important was that he achieved a healthy balance with the *important things* at the right time. This can mean sacrificing in some areas but it really won't feel that way because you are prospering in other areas; that is why you remove the negative forces so that you are only selecting between positive choices.

I remember as an undergraduate student deciding that graduating with a "B" average was "ok" with me because my social life (a positive one) was just as important at that time. Since my mother had died a couple of years prior to my college entry, my dad lived on the other side of the world, my brother in the Navy and my dysfunctional family in Brooklyn, I felt I needed that college "family." My emotional needs were being met through my affiliation with various organizations and that was just as important to me as my academic needs so I worked to achieve a healthy balance between the two. I wanted to hang out with my sorority sisters, go to parties and then hang out some more...I didn't want to be "that chick" that studied all night and missed out on all social engagements in pursuit of her degree. I sacrificed some "A's" in courses for some "A's" in relationships because my inner soul needed to be fulfilled...Remember, I still felt that hole in my heart and soul since my mother died and I was trying everything to fill it. I had great professional aspirations and I knew I had to work hard to get there but I also knew that this hole within me needed to be filled for my emotional aspirations also so I balanced the two. Was this the right move? Hmmmm....I think so because I was able to cultivate relationships that I still maintain today...25+ years.

I am a stronger woman because of these experiences and it helped me to balance out other important aspects of my life. Your task is deciding what the balance may be between and to eliminate the negative choices so that you only focus on the positive selections. Remember, you have to decide what the healthy balance is for you. You have to consistently "check your gauge" to ensure that you are operating at the right levels. Check your emotional gauge...is it level to your physical gauge? Aligned with your school gauge? Relationship gauges? Or, is there an imbalance somewhere? It becomes your responsibility to ensure that it all balances out to a level of comfort that works for your life and the lives of those who are the closet to you. Checking your gauge at least twice monthly to achieve the healthy balance is extremely important to *Go Hard* and *Get Over It!*

Sample Healthy Balance Gauge

(emotional, academics, relationships, physical)

PART IV

A= ANGER AND ARTILLERY TO *GET OVER IT!*

Do you know exactly what pisses you off? When was the last time you wrote a list detailing the things that make you angry? Those things that can "take you over the edge" and make you feel like you can destroy the world with your anger and make you stumble hard? Well, you need to know this so you can really "check yourself" when situations occur that can lead to your anger emerging inappropriately. Keep in mind that although I think that anger is a healthy emotion it can also be destructive and frightening. There are a plethora of folks occupying jail cells because of their anger and not knowing how to control it. It's what you do with the anger that makes a difference and dealing with anger is an enormous task that many of us struggle with our entire lives. Anger is a controlling emotion that can take us "out of ourselves" and serve as our own destructive mechanism. If we don't get a grip on what makes us angry then we will not be equipped to deal with the anger once it begins to emerge. What do I do? How do I try to deal with those folks and situations that just piss me off? I usually ask myself the following questions prior to "allowing" myself to become *really* angry.

Step 1*:*   Ask yourself "what is really happening here?" *Gather* the facts.

Step 2:   Who is involved? Are they even important in my life? Do they make a daily difference in my life? *Understand* your feelings about the facts.

Step 3:   Do I really care? Some things are annoying but are they really worth the emotional drain that anger causes my body? *Analyze (break it down)* the effect.

Step 4: If I care, then *WHY* do I really care? Is it about my feelings getting hurt? Are folks trying to take advantage of me? What is it about this situation that I really care about? *Evaluate (judge the significance)* the situation.

Step 5: How will my anger affect all parties? What will the combined effect be? How will it affect other areas in my life? *Synthesize (combine the elements)* the effect.

Step 6: Just how am I going to deal with the situation that made me angry? After taking steps 1-5 above, I really need to decide on a plan of action.

Cussing out folks is rarely an option so I have to determine if I will just let my anger subside and then approach the situation rationally or if I will just let it go. I usually decide if I will just "let it go" based upon step 3 (analyze the effect). If I really don't care, then it is a completed anger moment. But if I really do care, then I move on to steps 4 and, 5 (evaluate the situation, synthesize the effect, create a plan of action). There is no blueprint for dealing with anger because each situation is different with varied individuals as the root causes. What you can create is a "popcorn" response to buy you some time to figure the situation out.

A "popcorn" response reflects the emotions that you display when the anger initially emerges. Like the popcorn bag in the microwave it starts off a bit slow but within a minute the kernels begin to pop faster and the bag begins to swell. If you don't watch the time and listen carefully to the pace of the kernels popping you could burn your popcorn. Your anger works in the same way. It may start off slow as you try to "get a grip" on the situation but can easily begin to swell if you do not control it. If you do not create a plan of action to avoid the anger kernels from overheating your frustration can continue to grow until it burns. When anger burns, we feel it throughout our bodies; our throats feel scorched because we can never get the words out the way we want to. Our heart rate increases so we begin to feel a shortness of breath. Our face becomes tense because it takes more muscles to frown than smile and in some cases our heads begin to hurt because our blood pressure has risen as a result of the anger. To avoid this experience, we need a popcorn response that is realistic and will work for us.

Dealing with anger requires that we know who has the power to make us angry. Once we reach step 3 and decide that we need to move on to step 4 we have to implement the plan of action. Popcorn responses may include:

1. Choosing to walk away from the physical situation, the surroundings causing the anger
2. Listening to music that soothes our souls
3. Drawing
4. Meditating
5. Writing about our anger
6. Singing
7. Exercising
8. Praying
9. Talking to someone who will actually care and listen

I actually go on "shut down" and remove myself from the situation that is causing the anger but I also write. I have a collection of poems that I have written during my lifetime that reflect angry moments. Or, you may choose to talk to someone who will actually listen and will not push the microwave buttons that force your anger kernels to pop faster. Whatever your popcorn response is you need it in life to control your anger. It won't make the situation go away but at least it can buy you some time to think before you act and make yourself stumble harder. You know, "hesitate" before you instigate or aggravate! *Going Hard* doesn't mean that you have to "Go Angry." I had to learn that the hard way and lost a bit of myself along the way.

I discovered the depth of my anger as a 17 year old college freshman. For years, I used to think that I had it all in control…that despite all of the negative things that happened in my life I was able to control myself emotionally so I really didn't allow myself to get angry. I always seemed to rationalize behavior first so that I wouldn't get to that level of anger. What I missed, however, was my "popcorn response" so I had no idea of what to do and how to respond once I really was angry because basically I had never really allowed myself to get to that point as a teenager. Well, I learned as a college freshman that if something touches my soul, challenges my healthy existence or messes with my mind, I can get dangerously angry and it could cost me the very thing that I was angry about to begin with.

When I first went to college it was so important for me to be accepted by my peers. Growing up in my household with my mother and grandmother I had some feelings of inferiority, as though I could never be "good enough" and live up to their expectations. I constantly tried to gain their approval and didn't always feel successful so I would look on the outside of our home for validation. Yes, I knew that they loved me but I just felt that they *liked* my brother more. So as that college freshman, it was important for me to be in the "in" group so that I could feel wanted, liked, loved and accepted.

I wanted to be a part of a group called the Alpha Angels. They were the "little sisters" to the brothers of Alpha Phi Alpha Fraternity Inc. and I desperately wanted to become an "Angel." At the time there were specific tasks that we had to do before our initiation and part of it was writing down the tasks in the "Halo" book and receiving instructions from the girls who were already Angels at that time. It just stopped short of being an actual pledge process used in black sororities at the time but I wanted it soooo badly. I saw a "family" in the form of this fraternity and Alpha Angel sisterhood and I desperately needed to be a part of it so when one of the "big sisters" deliberately and perhaps maliciously interfered with my goal (she took my Halo book and wouldn't give it back), I became extremely angry…out of control angry. That anger led to me actually punching her in the mouth. OUCH! Yep, I did it and at the moment it felt soooo good but within 30 seconds I knew that I was out of control so I ran. I just ran out of the dorm, down the four flights of stairs and continued to run for about a mile. I sat at the bus stop for about an hour but the irony was that the bus had stopped running and I knew that but I just sat there. I finally checked into a motel and I was emotionally and mentally exhausted. I needed to rest so I could figure out how I would deal with the consequences of my actions.

I remember being scared. Scared of what the next day would bring and scared of what would happen to me because of my anger and my actions. But most of all I was scared of myself. I needed to figure how I would deal with the consequences of my actions. I was scared of myself because I had never been a violent person other than in situations where I had to physically defend myself against my peers as a younger child (I used to get in some physical fights with other girls) but now I was the initiator of the attack! I was actually the attacker! I questioned the very essence of who I was, what I believed in, and I couldn't figure out why I actually punched her when I served as my mother's punching bag for so many years. I knew what it felt like to be hit, to be beaten and to stare in shock after it actually happened. I was a terrified and alone 17 year old girl hiding out in a motel room because of my uncontrollable anger.

I learned from that experience that bottling anger only makes it stronger, ignoring anger only camouflages it and expressing anger is a delicate skill. It was a lesson that I knew I had to learn so it was after this incident that I began thinking about my "popcorn response." I knew that I needed a plan of action to control the anger that would return if other important things in my life were threatened.

Several relationships were strained as a result of my actions (punching the "big sister") and the organization "took sides." Some of the members empathized with my actions but others looked at my behavior with disdain. It was a complicated, confusing and hurtful time of my life and I still remember the vulnerability I felt while going through it. I felt like I had stumbled in the darkness and could not find my way to the light awaiting me at the top of the emotional pit of heartache and turmoil. In the end I did become an Alpha Angel but was gently reminded of the result of my anger through jokes such as being called "Joe Frazier" and continually being questioned about it in various situations.

I grew up in an environment where you were expected to fight for yourself if you believed you were wronged. It was "okay" to punch someone in the face if they disrespected you or treated you unfairly. In fact, my mother taught me that if someone even "looked like they wanted to do something" I should "pick up the nearest thing to me and bust their heads wide open." Wowwww....I saw my mom physically fight another woman, her brother and vaguely and incident with my father. Yes, I grew up fighting all the time...sometimes two fights in one day because I just wouldn't give up. I won some but lost many but the point was made that no one was going to walk all over me and if you did me wrong then there were consequences you had to pay....What a horrific way to deal with my anger.

After the incident with the "big sister" I knew that I never, ever, wanted to endure this again and that my anger was a sign of vulnerability that I needed to control. Because of this I began creating the blueprint of my popcorn response in the fall of 1982 and through my life's experiences I created my completed popcorn response:

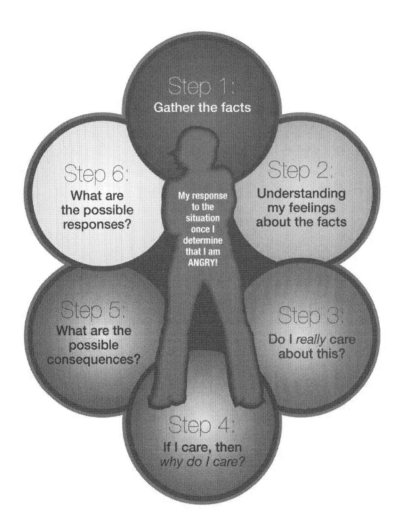

Sample Popcorn Response

It includes knowing those things that can make you angry, figuring out your popcorn response and then putting that response into action when the situations arise. You have to protect yourself but I am not convinced that anger is the best method of protection.

Instead, build your arsenal of weapons to protect what is sacred in your heart. That would be your artillery.

Artillery:

Artillery is used to combat your own weapons of personal destruction and any abuse by others that you may experience. Find out what your stumbling blocks are that can destroy you emotionally and psychologically, and then build your strategic plan to combat the battle against them. *NOTHING* should be able to break you spiritually though! You should begin building your artillery each time you are hurt and feel discouraged. It can be done initially by keeping an audio journal, written journal, notes, etc. and "talking" yourself through the pain. Try to get in touch with who you are when you are hurt and frustrated. What did you do the last time this level of anger occurred? What did you do daily to function? Did you turn to God for strength and wisdom? Did you listen to specific songs that appeared to be speaking directly to you and your situation? Or, did you read motivational passages and find inspiration from those? What exactly did you do? How did you pull yourself out of that "black hole" you dug for yourself or were thrown in? Make note of the specific actions so that you can use these healing mechanisms as your artillery when you are faced with your next hurt. Yes, your next hurt…it comes with living a full life and becoming a responsible adult. Folks are not earmarked just to be hurt because I believe we live in a world of opposites and you cannot have one without other. There is no joy without pain but it is how we cope with it that determines the winners and the losers…those who are the foot soldiers which emerge from the trenches of despair or those who will be buried under the corpse of pain.

My life has definitely been wrought with pain and suffering and I have spent a significant amount of time building my artillery to protect it but I feel stronger after each hurt. I recognize that it definitely takes a higher level/degree to pierce my heart and soul now. The ironic thing is that my deadliest weapon is the (feeling/emotion) of "indifference." I've learned that it's often a case of "mind over matter." As much as I mind is as much as it will matter. And, if I don't mind, then it definitely won't matter. In other words, "don't sweat the small stuff." Don't borrow worries. Many things that I experienced in my life just don't matter anymore so they cannot hurt me. This includes my personal and my professional life. I do what I have to do so I can do what I want to do and I don't get involved in many things that won't allow me to do what I want to do. Make sense? Let me say it again so that you clearly follow me: *"I do what I have to do so I can do what I want to do and I don't get involved in many things that won't allow me to do what I want to do."* It took me a long time to learn that staying in my lane helps in the protection of everything in my square that I talked about earlier. I simply "don't borrow worries" anymore because if I did then my "wants" can be threatened.

How did I do this and what did I do? How did I learn to protect myself? At an early age I learned to "mask" my emotions to move forward and I still do it today. Depending on the expectations, I wear different "hats" and "masks" daily. I learned how to "play the game" where I pretend that you haven't hurt me and ignore the initial "wound" but after analyzing the situation I may need to address any pain that you may have actually inflicted. You see I handle situations by ensuring that I don't put Band-Aids on gunshot wounds. I perform the surgery and sometimes it can be a long and grueling process but nevertheless I gather my artillery and I come out "shooting" to protect my heart, my soul, my spirit and my family. I learned how to do this at a young age; to disguise pain and abuse as indifference and camouflage heartache as fictional.

Smiling and pretending like I care…

So underneath my skin are an actress and a surgeon who lives without fear of tomorrow. She thrives to be able to look in the mirror and not think "when I look into the mirror there isn't anyone looking back at me." And she knows that she is indeed a strong and smart girl with the potential of omnipotence…She couldn't depend on her positive self-esteem from others so she had to begin the process of "digging deep" for herself and creating a plan that she would use to increase her artillery. She can *Get Over It!* because she can protect what is important in her life by using her heart, soul and her mind to build her artillery.

<u>Mind paralysis</u>

A mind that is paralyzed is synonymous with a body without a soul.

It simply doesn't function.

It limits the ability to critically think, analyze and grow. It presents as an empty shell

And then the heart is affected as well. What causes the mind to freeze?

To think that it can process whatever it pleases? Blame it the culture, environment, or alcohol? Nah, I don't think that's it…no, not at all…. Instead, for many it is a chosen ignorance

Where folks forget to be done of negative vibes…good riddance! There are some who love to wallow in their own self-indulgence. Just stay away from them…the odor of negativity is pungent! Only wrap your mind around things that work

And embrace the things that just don't hurt

Don't let your mind play a checkers game with little need to concentrate

When the strength of your thoughts will allow you to play chess and scream "Checkmate!"

Ahhh, a mind that is paralyzed is synonymous to a body without a soul

And a mind paralyzed is like a rotary phone

Decrepit and old.

Using a "SWOT" analysis can be helpful at this point in order to assess what is happening in your world and see what you need to build your arsenal for/against. This is a strategic plan typically used by businesses to evaluate the Strengths, Weaknesses, Opportunities and Threats (SWOTs) of the business. Its creation is credited to Albert Humphrey and it is primarily used to move toward change[ii]. I think that it is relevant to our lives and experiences because when we evaluate our own lives to move toward change these are the areas that we need to focus on to make the changes.

Strengths focuses on what we are good at and the good things in our lives...those things that inspire us and keep us dreaming and hoping and knowing that "Yes, we can!" These are the characteristics/things in our lives that can place us at an advantage over us to help others to achieve our goals.

Weaknesses are the exact opposite of our strengths because these are the characteristics/things that slow our growth and development. These qualities/obstacles/stumbling blocks can prohibit us from developing into positive beings and submerges our productive thoughts and activities under a concrete slab of negativity. What type of waste is in your life now? What are your weaknesses that you are aware of? Who are the "weak" people that you allow to remain in your life?

Opportunities focus on those external chances that you may receive to make a positive difference in your life. How many times have you passed on an opportunity because of doubt or fear? I think we miss good opportunities in our lifetimes because we have a fear of the unknown and the fear of failure. We would rather live in a "comfortable hell" (as my friend Tre says) than reach out and take a chance in an "uncomfortable heaven." We often get too comfortable in our skin and our environments that we live in a victim's mentality and will not seize the opportunity to move toward positive change in our lives.

If you are going to *Get Over It! and Go Hard* then you have to at least take advantage of some of the opportunities that may come your way. I'm not one to jump on every "change train" that rattles by but I know that there have been several instances that I felt that no one ever gave me anything but a chance and I took that opportunity and ran with it. If that was all I was offered then that is what I would take. For example, my high school grades were horrendous…not because I wasn't smart but basically because I never went to class my freshman and sophomore years. I wanted to hang out all day in cafeteria with my friends who liked me and accepted me for who I was. I felt like a "regular" teenager hanging with them and not the scared, worthless girl that I felt when I went home to St. Marks Ave. My grades sucked and I really wasn't eligible to attend many of the four year schools that I wanted to but I had a role model at the time, Leilani, who went to a small Catholic college in upstate New York who felt I had a chance there.

Leilani was everything that I wanted to be…smart, cute and tough. She seemed confident and assured about her future and her life appeared to be a happy life. I wanted to be just like her so when she suggested that I come up to her college for a visit with her sister (Danielle and I were best friends anyway) I jumped at the chance. She told me to bring a copy of my transcript and she helped to arrange an interview with admissions for me. Once I arrived I had my interview with admissions, told them the story of my life and the impact it had on my first two years of high school. They listened carefully and then escorted me to a program that was designed to assist kids such as myself who had academic deficiencies but had great potential. I interviewed with that program director, was accepted and I enrolled in Daemen College in June, 1982. They gave me the chance and I took it.

You see, there were people who could only offer me a chance but it was my responsibility to accept the opportunity. That's what opportunity is all about. God can definitely bless you with talent but if you don't take the opportunity to "grow" that talent then it is basically a talent wasted. As you continue to work on your self-directed search, don't forget to take advantage of some opportunities along the way.

Threats…Be wary of these because they represent those challenges to your opportunities, dreams and to your sanity. These are the external elements that can threaten your progress and seek to destroy your dreams. I think this is where you will need your artillery as well. You need to be prepared at all times for those things and those people who only wish the worst for you. What will be your plan of action? Hmmmm…be wary of yourself too, sometimes we can be our own worst enemy because we live in that comfortable hell. I know all about it through the way I deal with my finances.

It's important to create your own SWOT analysis and the following diagram was created to give you a visual of what it could look like. Be honest as you create it because you know what I said about lying to yourself….To *Get Over It!* you have to know how to *Go Hard* and the SWOT analysis helps you to do that.

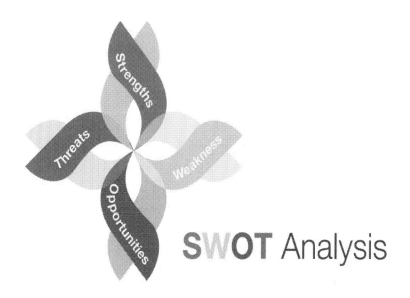

PART V

R= REMEMBRANCE, RESILIENCE, RESTORATION, RENEWAL, RIGHTEOUSNESS TO *GET OVER IT!*

Remembrance:

"Lest we forget..." How can we forget? We certainly have learned how to forgive but oh, can we really forget? It's like we really don't have control over this physiological aspect of lives. But we do have control over what we do with our memories. Will we allow them to haunt us? Force us to live in an emotional ditch of anger and negativity? Or, will we take those memories and use them as the impetus for change for our emotional, spiritual and intellectual growth? For the cultivation of new perspectives knowing what doesn't work? Well, I honestly think that it is a combination of all of these variables. I would love to forget the days when I was abused in different circumstances. I would like to erase the painful memories from the core of my existence but if I did that, then how could I have learned some of my life's lessons? How could I know what can hurt me and how to really find the elusive pot of gold at the end of the rainbow?

I remember "Mr. Dum Dum" who worked at the Puerto Rican bodega around the corner from where I lived as a child. My mother had "credit" there so she always sent me around the corner with the list to get the food and she would pay later...at least she thought she would. I feel as though I paid the price when he would take me to the backroom and explore my body parts. Mr. Dum Dum did make me feel so special...he told me how pretty and how smart I was because I could add up the cost of all the groceries in my head and he didn't have to do it. He would smile as soon as I would walk in and I felt so important because I believed that he thought I was special…I know now that I was just a child trying to find love and herself in all of the wrong places…in search of rainbows with pots of gold at the end of them. I was 9 years old.

While there have been several other encounters in my life where I have been violated there is one that I am willing to share with you because I was a teenager at the time and I thought I had all of the answers (as typical teens do). I should have known better than to go on a date with a guy I worked my summer job with, Clarence, and should have followed my "instincts." When I met him downtown Brooklyn and he had a leather vest on with no shirt on in the middle of July (ewwww!) that should have been my first clue because he did not present himself as the typical guy I dated. We were supposed to go to the movies but for whatever reason we ended up walking from downtown Brooklyn all the way back to my house (a few miles). We talked, laughed and had a good time that night so I didn't think anything of it the next day when he asked if I just wanted to come over and "chill" at his crib. So, I jumped on the train and headed toward his house with my shorts and belly shirt on (I was 18 at the time). He introduced me to his granddad downstairs and we went upstairs…all was well as we watched TV and then he started smoking weed and snorting cocaine that was on his dresser.

I wanted to play the grown, street smart woman so I pretended that I was around this type of activity all of the time so I continued to watch the television as he did his drugs. Although I had never done drugs myself or smoked weed, I had been around many of my cousins and some friends who did. That part really was no big deal to me…it was watching someone snort coke that was new.

Shortly after taking his drugs he tried to "get close" with me and I really refused his advances because the attraction just wasn't there.

He actually turned me off with his sweaty armpits, drippy jheri-curled hair and musty body odor. At that point I was ready to go home and I told him so. He stared at me as though I was a foreign object and said that I wasn't going anywhere. What? You've got to be kidding me! I worked with this dude every day in my summer job and I thought I had a good grasp of his character but I didn't. He pushed me down on the bed with his full weight…I slapped him, and with all of the power of my 114 pound body I tried to push him away and off of me. He began pulling down my shorts and panties and I kept fighting…he reached over and pulled out a cutlass from either the nightstand or under the bed. While holding the cutlass to my neck with one hand he was able to take my shorts off and force himself on me…How gross was that?

I was raped that night and I felt that I was no longer strong…I let the concept of being strong go and began to beg for him to just let me go. I told him "Clarence, I don't deserve this…I only wanted to be your friend." I tried to leave but he blocked the door but as he looked at me his eyes had softened. As though it were a different man than five minutes prior…I had to think fast to get out of there…I had to get away…"What to do?" "What do you say?" Ah-ha! "Clarence, please let me go to the bathroom to clean myself up. I have to use the bathroom and I can't do it here." He looked at me again, and moved aside but he still somewhat blocked the doorway leading downstairs and outside to my freedom. I went in the bathroom, wiped myself off with wet toilet paper and then peeked outside of the door…Clarence was bending over tying his shoe laces. Without a second thought I "made a break for it." I practically jumped over him, ran downstairs, swung open the front door and kept running the 3 long blocks toward the train station.

When I arrived at the train station, out of breath and quite disheveled, I realized that I had left my change purse that had my house keys attached to it. There was a transit cop there whom I begged to let me go under the turnstile...at first he said "no" but after seeing the desperation and tears in my eyes he said "Go ahead sweetheart." I clearly remember his face when he said it. I ran upstairs and at that precise moment the train came and I jumped on it...My ride to freedom.

I felt so ashamed, I was afraid and I felt dirty. It was embarrassing. And, who would actually believe me? Didn't I bring this on myself? Was this what they defined as "rape?" Was this a "date rape?" What was it? I was so confused...I did not tell a few people years later the extent of what happened that night nor did I report it to any authority figure because in my mind it was partially my fault. So it's been about three decades and I still believe that I played a dangerous game that night and I lost. I think I saw Clarence once more after that episode at work. I remember being speechless and terrified when I saw him so I asked another manager if I could go home because I didn't feel well. Shortly after that Clarence was moved to another shift and then I went back to college so our paths never really crossed again. I will always, always, remember the demonic, crazed look that he gave me as he entered me and held me down with the cutlass. Yes, it was a dangerous game that I will always remember and I knew I had to deal with the consequences.

How did I do this? I measured the consequences against the abuse I had previously endured and figured if I could "get over" those ills then there wasn't much in my life that I couldn't get through. But do we really have to go this painful distance to learn valuable lessons? Just as the thorn bird spends its life trying to find the longest, sharpest spine to impale itself on; do we as human continuously seek out people who will hurt us? Searching for people whom we know does not have our best interests at the forefront? Who are wrong for our spirits and well-beings? We know that these people have the power to hurt us but yet we seek them out and we love them anyway. Why do we allow these people in our lives that only want to see us stumble? Why?

Sometimes we hold on to negative memories just a bit too long and we let them dictate how we feel today. We fail to take those memories and use them as motivators for our continued growth and allow ourselves to "move on." It becomes somewhat easier to "hold on" to negative memories then to create new positive thoughts. So at what point do we begin to let memories be just that...memories? How do we move away from those stumbling blocks and move towards building our own resiliency to fight against the pain of remembering those hurtful things and instead begin on our path of righteousness and renewal? We have to do that...we have chosen the slides that we are going to include in our memory PowerPoint presentations. To Get Over It! you have to select those slides that will only empower you...not endanger you.

Resilience:

Becoming resilient is not an easy feat because you have to build a "thicker skin" and stronger backbone to stand firm against the hurricane force winds of change that will happen in your life. For me, I always believed that it starts from within...knowing what I was going to battle for and gauging how strong I needed to be. I would look at how important the issue was and how much artillery I would need to fight. Once I had my arsenal in line then I would feel strong, with that strength I felt resilient and have been able to battle emotional and sexual abuse, racism, classism and Lupus for the majority of my life. Sometimes I've been more resilient than others but I never, ever, just walk away and give up. You have to decide how far you are willing to go...how tenacious you will be to protect your investment.

As a teenager I had to be resilient just to survive....You see, after Ma died I was a bit lost...I knew that my life would be different and I actually felt "free" because things seemed to settle down around me and Mom Belk and I had created a new life for ourselves. We moved into a 2 bedroom apartment that was not roach and mice infested. I finally had my own bedroom and my Uncle Marsh had given us decent furniture and beds to sleep on. It was a "peaceful" existence but I still struggled for significance due to my uncertainty of my future. I always had dreams but wasn't convinced of the path I needed to follow to achieve those dreams. My resiliency served as the backbone to allow me to keep trying different avenues to lead me down that road to prosperity…I needed a sane mind and the ability to "let go" of so much of that negative past in order to move forward. I had to *Get Over It!* and that resiliency is what allowed me to "bounce back" after all of the setbacks…I had decided how far I wanted to go in life and that I would invest everything that I had to get there and to protect my investment…I knew that I had my artillery and faith in order and the future was simply awaiting my arrival. Being a teenager did not excuse me from my responsibility for securing a successful future for myself nor was it a crutch for me to use to explain destructive behavior…

Keep in mind though, that everything is not important or relevant so you will have to carefully select your battles while remembering not to borrow worries. You have to find that strength in you to remain resilient in the echoes of the "no's" and use that strength to move you towards restoration.

Beneath the valves

Where do you find strength?

In the valves of a broken heart?

Or, in the soles of feet that stand strong?

Where is that extra "umph" that you so desperately need when you can hear the sound of a silent tear?

Where is the commander in chief of your spirit when you feel as though you are no longer that foot soldier who can emerge from the trenches of despair?

How can you make the empty hole inside of you feel fulfilled?

Should you call the builder of tranquility? The architect of "peace, love and harmony?

Or, can you do it yourself?

Strength probably lies beneath the pain and layers of frustration, Way below the confusion and under the pillars of disbelief.

Can you still find yourself?

Or, is the "me" lost underneath other significant issues in your life? How do you move on?

How do you get along?

How do you smile when you really want to sigh? What do you do to just get by?

Will you discover the armor to protect your soul? Or will you simply continue to do spiritual patrol? Where is the strength?

How deep can it be?

Better yet, why is it such a mystery?

I used to be so strong….look at what you have done to me.

Or, have I done it to myself? Is this my reality?

I can't find it, can't find myself, can't find me no more…. It's like it ran out on me…through an open door.

Where do you find strength?

In the valves of a broken heart?

Or should you look for it in the decisions you make or roads you travel as a start?

Strength, yes, which used to define me.

But now, where is that woman, her heart and her soul that used to be?

Ahhhh, there she is…cuddled way down below,

Just trying to figure out where her rock, her pillar of strength is……does anybody know?

Once you have remembered the positive experiences in your life and have determined when and how you are going to be resilient, then I think that you can begin to move onto the path of *restoration, renewal and righteousness*. You can begin to restore those deep, dark areas in your heart and soul that have been previously damaged. You cannot get there to do this if you have not remembered the positive and negative coupled with the associated challenges.

Restoration:

I really believe that if you are going to stumble, then as you are stumbling, still try to balance yourself and stumble forward…in the direction of *restoration*. To begin the *restoration* process you need a goal of where you want to be. It cannot simply be "I just don't want to hurt anymore." Instead, it should represent what you *don't* want to feel, where you *don't* want to be and where you *don't* want to go. This requires honesty about who you are, how you function and that requires us to look deep within in and acknowledge our faults that we spend many waking hours running away from, sugarcoating and denying their existence. But to begin to restore our inner spirits and renew our faith in ourselves we have to be honest with ourselves. Folks ask me all the time "how do you do it all?" And I often respond "I don't think about it…I'm like Nike because I just do it." Well, I do it because I spend time critically evaluating and analyzing myself -- self-reflection. I take the good, the bad and the ugly about myself and I synthesize what it all means as a total person. I try to look at myself through the eyes of others to understand what they see in me and how they view who I am. To do this I have to be able to embrace honesty. Once I am honest with myself I can lead myself along the path of restoration, renewal and righteousness.

The term *restoration* is defined as "the return of something that was removed or abolished." I really think that your faith plays an enormous role here. I believe that having faith in the possibilities and your dream will allow you to begin restoring what was removed from your life that may have limited those possibilities.

Ma died when I was 14, it really took a long time for me to truly "love again." I honestly don't think that I loved unconditionally again until my oldest son was born. Ma's death took such an emotional toll on me that I had blocked my heart from feeling that deep about anybody or anything. It was a jail of loneliness that I sentenced myself to because I felt that was the only way to protect myself from being hurt again. I was so afraid of losing something I loved so much again that I decided if I didn't love so hard then I wouldn't lose so hard. I removed my ability to love unconditionally and replaced it with my ability to intellectualize and internalize everything. It took the birth of my son and the nurses coming into my hospital room a day after he was born to take him from me for me to begin my restoration process.

In January 1986 at the age of 20 I learned that I had Lupus which is an autoimmune disease that transcends across race, class, gender and socioeconomics. It is a "silent" disease because it attacks each person differently and it is actually a combination of symptoms that lead doctors to test patients for Lupus. These symptoms can include but are not limited to:

- extreme fatigue (tiredness) headaches
- painful or swollen joints
- fever
- anemia (low numbers of red blood cells or hemoglobin, or low total blood volume)
- swelling (edema) in feet, legs, hands, and/or around eyes
- pain in chest on deep breathing (pleurisy)
- butterfly-shaped rash across cheeks and nose
- sun- or light-sensitivity (photosensitivity)
- hair loss
- abnormal blood clotting
- fingers turning white and/or blue when cold (Raynaud's phenomenon)
- mouth or nose ulcers

It was a difficult time in my life because I couldn't understand where I had contracted this disease. The uncertainty about the origin of the disease weighed on my mind heavily because I didn't know what my prognosis would be. But since I had learned by that point to embrace positivity I knew that I had to "keep it moving" in spite and despite of this diagnosis. So I moved forward in marrying, successfully becoming pregnant, engaging in an exciting but high risk pregnancy and then delivering my son after the labor was induced. I thought that if I had my babies as soon as possible then I would have more time to spend with them if my disease became life-threatening or fatal as I aged. I simply didn't know and I don't think that the doctors really knew at that time either that my son could be in jeopardy of being afflicted by the disease as an infant. So my husband and I made the conscientious decision to begin our family from the onset of our marriage. I had no idea, however, that my son would become sick from the Lupus antibodies in my bloodstream and his life would be threatened the moment he was born.

My soul felt so empty when they took my baby away as we lay next to each other in our hospital room that night. I remember laying on my right side with him cuddled against my chest as he was swaddled in his hospital issued white blanket with the blue and pink trim. The fluorescent light over the bed was on and he was just lying there staring at it. His eyes were a grayish blue color at that time, and he was so fair skinned with "wisps" of hair but I kept thinking "this baby is so beautiful and he is MINE!" So as we were cuddling the nurse came in and announced that my baby had to immediately go to the intensive care unit (ICU) because his blood work was abnormal and he needed a blood transfusion. *WHAT?* A blood transfusion? Seriously? He's only a day old! Why can't he just have *MY* blood? She informed me that it was *because* of my blood that he was sick. I sat up in the bed, dazed and confused as she picked up my baby, gently placed him in the portable bassinet and rolled him away to ICU. Before she left she did indicate that the doctors would come into my room in a few minutes to explain everything to me. Wow!

When they wheeled me down to the intensive care unit (ICU) unit (I wasn't able to walk yet after the birth) and I saw him as he lay in that incubator with a needle sticking out of his forehead I gasped! He was swaddled quite tightly in his blanket but he looked as though he was in a lot of pain and he had a look of "bewilderment" on his face…as though he were searching for that fluorescent light that he stared at while he lay with me. I felt helpless…at that moment I felt like I couldn't do anything to help him. He looked like a little ragdoll that doubled as a pin cushion because of all the needle pricks he had in the heels of his little feet and I couldn't protect him. My baby was 1 day old and only 6 pounds living in the ICU and no one could give me a definitive diagnosis or prognosis. What could I do? What did I need to do? I didn't quite understand medically what was happening and emotionally it just didn't make sense. What I did know, however, was that although I only knew my son for one day, the love I had for him felt as though I loved him for my entire life. I knew that he needed me and he needed to feel my love. At that moment that was all that I had in order to help him and the only way he could feel the love I had inside was if it were unconditional love. It did not matter that he had medical issues, he was my son and he was my gift from God to take care of…unconditionally. I had to find that depth of love that I felt for my own mother and use it for my son. I knew that there was a powerful bond between mother and child and I needed that bond to *immediately* emerge. How could I get to it since I had not allowed myself to *love hard* since Ma's death? I knew I had to restore what was lost…I had to.

I began by praying and through this prayer I began releasing my pain of the loss of my mother and began restoring my own ability to love so I could love my baby unconditionally *and* so that he could *feel* that love. I had to do it because my son needed me *and* I needed him. We needed each other and his survival was dependent on this unconditional love. Through this pain and emotional upheaval, I had begun my restoration process and my prayers were answered when eventually the doctors were able to diagnosis his condition (neonatal Lupus) and began to see improvement in his condition. You see, answers to prayers can be immediate too.

As a result of my prayers and the power of positive thinking the ability to love unconditionally that I lost when Ma died had now been restored because I had my own child to love. I had to push through all of this pain to restore my ability to love unconditionally. I have to admit, that each time I think about that night it is still emotional for me because I don't think I have totally forgiven myself for not educating myself on the possibility of him becoming sick (that's another story for another day though!). What I do know is that to *Get Over It!* sometimes you have to *Go Hard* and *lose hard* (to feel the pain) in order to restore whatever it is that you have lost.

What do YOU need to restore?

Renewal:

Renewal is a part of moving toward righteousness because you must cleanse yourself of negativity first. It requires that you release that negative energy whether or not it comes from yourself or the people you surround yourself with. You will need to walk with a gait that is reflective of strength and not stumbling actions. You have to know how to forgive (as previously discussed) in order to renew because renewal is almost a cyclical process…what you put in, you get out. Garbage in equates to garbage out. Positivity breeds positivity. I believe that the renewal process is similar to the action research process in scientific, disciplined inquiry.

Action research is an interactive, reflective inquiry process that balances problem solving actions with positive behavior in an effort to understand underlying causes to enable future predictions about making changes. The ultimate goal is to move toward change and there are basically 6 steps:

1. *Find out*: Why are you beginning this process? Why do you feel the need to renew the things that make up your inner being?

2. *Make a plan*: How will I begin this renewal process? What are the things that I need to change in my life to begin cleansing my soul and my mind? This is an important step because it determines which direction your renewal process will take. This may take the longest time because you have to weigh the positive and

the negative and identify the consequences of every action.

3. *Make things happen*: I've been guilty of surrounding myself with people who "let things happen" in their lives and then I am the one to try to clean up their mess because I am one who "makes things happen." I firmly believe that after you "let go and let God," you have the responsibility of taking the opportunities/talents that God has bestowed upon you to move toward positive change. You cannot just simply sit there and expect good things to flow towards you…you have to get out there and take the steps to make things happen. This should be easier for you if you have a concrete plan of action (as discussed in #2).

4. *Listen:* Listening can often be a difficult task for us. We may hear what others are saying to us but are we really listening? Especially when they are saying things that we really do not want to hear. And we all know that the truth hurts when it is based upon flaws in our character. In order to renew our faith, our souls and our belief systems we have to listen to what we are being told by those who love and care about us. We have to listen to the word of God…the stories he uses to teach us. We need to listen to our own inner voices that often tell us when something is awry but we choose to ignore our intuition when it doesn't appear to be concrete and clear. Yes, listening is a skill that we need to renew ourselves.

5. *Think:* The process of critically thinking and analyzing our situation is a necessary and required

component of the renewal process. We have to be able to analyze, synthesize and evaluate the circumstances that led us on the journey of renewal. If we don't think about it then our renewal process becomes null and void because we will continue doing the same things but expect different results.

6. *Changing your plan*: Now that you have made a plan, made changes to your thought process, listened and critically thought about significant issues in your life you should be able to move towards change. I honestly think the reason people struggle with change in their lives is because they move too quickly. They react based upon emotional responses instead of the comprehensive review of the situation. If you looked at the issues from all angles then you can move toward making changes to improve your life situation. If you haven't explored all options then you are cheating yourself out of real change and self-renewal.

Sample Action Plan

Righteousness:

Hmmmm...I don't have a lot to explain about this other than if you don't refrain from being judgmental of others then you can't possibly think that your way of life is the only way to live. You won't believe that you are the only person who can be right and reject any and all constructive criticism in an effort to support your self-righteousness. Sometimes you are just wrong. Dead wrong and you need to remember that there is no self-righteousness in wrongness.

Wrong is just wrong. And, don't forget that two wrongs definitely don't equal a right so there are times when you are wronged you just need to "walk away" but still remain firm in your convictions. Just because you may not be able to say how you feel all the time doesn't mean that you don't feel it. Being always right doesn't always make you righteous…it just makes you right. While the former may feel good, it is the latter that will lead you to walk in the footsteps of God's words. And, as a theological concept, righteousness requires that your actions are justified and you lead a life pleasing to God…it doesn't mean that you just have to be "right." Hmmmm…how righteous are you *really?*

PART VI

D= DREAMS, DEPTH, DESTINY TO *GET OVER IT!*

Dreams:

Sometimes I have to search the deepest crevices in my soul to decide what I need to dream about next. Life can get so complacent, routine and mundane that there are times when I can get caught up in what *needs* to be done that I forget about what dreams *can* be done.

Dreams should serve as the motivation to the future just as your eyes serve as the mirror to your soul. They both should be the vision that you need to coherently feel. Without them you will spin around in that circle or get twisted around in a maze of despair. It's important to know what your dreams are for yourself – not just the dreams that your parents, family and friends have of you; or how to separate dreams that you may have for your own children from your own. You need distinguishable dreams for yourself that extend above and beyond the dreams of others so that you can feel fulfilled and remain intrinsically motivated.

I know that sometimes I lose myself and what I want in all of the sacrifices that I make and the dreams I have for my children and my marriage. I know that I am doing the right things for all of the right reasons but these things may not necessarily be for me. While this is not necessarily a bad thing, because when our children are safe, secure and happy we are generally happy, it is something that you have to gauge. If your dreams are consistently intertwined with the dreams of others than what happens if their dreams are deferred? What happens if their dreams do not become a reality? What do you do? Do you sacrifice your dreams to ensure that their dreams come true? Hmmmm....As a parent that's a tough one because I take my job as a parent very seriously and I know that God has only loaned me His children to take care of while on earth. I feel that if I don't use all of my resources to ensure that their dreams lead to prosperous reality then I am shortchanging them and not doing God's work. Perhaps this is what makes me that "helicopter" mom...you know, the one that hovers and swirls over their children's lives?

But you know what, I'm good with being that helicopter mom and I'm not going to apologize for it because if I am not protecting my children's hopes, dreams and rights then who will do it for them (besides their dad)? After all, these are God's children that I am protecting! The difference is, however, between me and another helicopter mom is that I still have my own dreams and I still believe in Santa Claus.

Santa Claus represents dreams to me because of all of the lessons that can be learned before he arrives Christmas evening. We learn that if we do good things and are good people then we can be rewarded ("You better watch out, you better not pout, you better not cry I'm telling you why..."). We learn that we can create our Christmas list and if the things that are on lists are realistic then Santa will grant our wish, bring our presents and fulfill our dreams. That's how life works to a degree. If we do the right things in life then we are typically rewarded. If we go to school, get good grades then we can get into good colleges to earn our degrees that will allow us to achieve personal goals and make our childhood dreams a reality. The irony to this example is that Santa *never* fulfilled my dreams as a child. I remember always having a Christmas list and *never* receiving anything on that list. I remember praying and praying and consistently doing the right things each year but Santa *never* gave me anything on my list. In fact, there were Christmases when Santa didn't even stop by our house on St. Marks. As I grew up I began to believe that the things that Santa brought me were not physical presents…they were virtues such as patience, faith and resiliency because as a child growing up in an abusive environment I needed those more than anything else in the world. I needed to keep believing that the "sun will come out tomorrow" and my patience would allow me to remain focused on my dreams of a safe and secure home of my own someday.

My dreams did become a reality and although it didn't happen overnight I worked my butt off to create a reality where my world was safe and secure. Now I'm not saying that it was okay to live as I did to get to this point but I am saying that sometimes you have to just keep dreaming. And when you finish one dream you move on to the next. I never stumbled so hard that I couldn't get back up and dream some more. I couldn't and wouldn't let that happen to me. *Never* stop dreaming and always have your own dreams…don't just piggyback off the dreams of others. If you have your own then that gives you something positive to think about on those nights when you are up, can't sleep and are twisting and turning. You can begin to think about the "what if's" of the dream and the steps that you need to make it a reality. See, the best part of dreams are you can make them what you want to. They can be complicated road maps to your successful future or they could be as simple as wanting to live a day pain-free as a Lupus patient. Either way, you control it…no one can give you a dream and no one can take the actual dream away from you…you own it and that's a powerful position to be in.

I remember as a young girl reading in a book that Ma gave to me about careers that Libras could find personal satisfaction in. It listed "milliner" as one of my choices but I had no idea what that was! I thought it was a misprint and it should have read "millionaire" so I was excited to know that I could be a millionaire and began to dream about what life like as such. It inspired me and it motivated me to believe that whatever I chose as my career path I really was destined to be a millionaire. Ah, the power of dreams!

I live and thrive on my dreams and sometimes although it is difficult to separate my dreams for my children from the dreams for myself, I do it and it still serves as that gentle reminder that Santa Claus *does* come to town and I can still be a dreamer.

Native Americans have traditionally used dream catchers. One of the old traditions was to hang a Dream Catcher in their homes. They believe that the night air is filled with dreams both good and bad. The Dream Catcher, when hung, moves freely in the air and catches the dreams as they float by. The good dreams know the way and slip through the center hole and slide down off the soft feathers so gently the sleeper below sometimes hardly knows he is dreaming. The bad dreams, not knowing the way, get entangled in the webbing and perish with the first light of the new day. The Ojibwa Indian Nation believes that a dream-catcher changes a person's dreams and that "Only good dreams would be allowed to filter through… Bad dreams would stay in the net, disappearing with the light of day."[iiii] I think that we should each have a dream-catcher to stop any negative dreams that may try to enter into our positive worlds and allow us to hold on to our positive dreams that we can make a reality. It does not necessarily have to be a replica of the Ojibwa Indian Nation's dream-catcher but some sort of symbol that we can recognize as our own instrument to collect our good dreams. Sometimes when I hear my neighbor's wind-chimes sounding on their back deck I think about my dreams blowing in the wind…

Depth:

Some folks have inferred that I take my life too seriously and that I take on too much responsibility. Friends and family have often encouraged me to "take it easy" and take care of myself. This is a challenge for me because I live so hard...my life has so much "depth" to it that many aspects require my attention daily. Although I do pick and choose what I will engage in daily sometimes the breadth of what appears on my list is overwhelming. I have to then narrow the focus and reassess my choices as to what is important. Some stuff simply doesn't get done...I embrace the *depth* of my involvement against the breadth of my activities and I really think that depth speaks volumes.

Some folks are just made to take it easy and therefore can just "let" life happen. I'm just not one of those folks and I have to pull things together to keep things together and to keep things moving along in a positive direction. This requires focuses on the depth of my commitment. I think that whatever you sign up to do you need to do it right or just don't do it at all. I know I get on folk's nerves because my expectation levels are pretty high but I really don't set them higher for anyone else than I set them for myself. You get out what you put in...garbage in, garbage out. Heart and soul in, heart and soul out. That's my expectation. That's what "depth" is all about...giving it your all and then you can expect "all" in return. The issue becomes perpendicular when you don't produce your best but you expect the best...Hmmmm...that's definitely an imbalance and I don't think there would be a true depth to your commitment if you did it that way.

What is YOUR depth level?

Destiny:

I think I have spent my lifetime trying to figure out exactly where my destiny is. I am always looking for that rainbow with the pot of gold at the end. Some days I think that I found the rainbow but when I look closely I only see a pile of rocks at the end of it.

This sends a signal to me that I have to continue trying and working harder because I'll need the strength to move that pile of rocks to the side in my quest to find my gold. I know that moving rocks is definitely not my destiny. And then there are other days when I reach the end of that rainbow and I see the pot glimmering and shining but when I get up close I realize that it is just the sun reflecting on glass...all that glitters is not gold. This tells me that I need to be careful of what I follow because there are a lot of fake people presenting fake situations and if I follow them then I am subject to only receiving "fool's gold." I'll tell you what though, most days I feel as though I am living in my pot of gold with my family. I feel so blessed that God has given me the opportunity to love and raise His children that I think my rainbow has ended in Powder Springs in Georgia and my home is actually my pot of gold...it's my destiny to be happy, safe and secure. This is where I really feel these things so I must have arrived at my true destiny. Hmmmm...

"Get Over It!" means to do everything from the core of your existence...it means not holding back and sucking in the final morsel of air to exhale confidently. You learn from your mistakes and use those mistakes as starting points change. Never embracing failure but knowing when to accept defeat. Understanding what makes you stumble but focusing on what makes you stronger. It means that you love hard, play hard, work hard, Mommy hard, wifey hard, sister hard and friend hard! You never skimp on challenges because you have invested your total self. This is the only way you can get over and get through things to keep it moving. You have to exercise your mind effectively because your brain power always serves as the impetus to move toward change. In this book I have focused on teaching you how to *"Get Over It!"* through the concepts aligned with the *"Go Hard"* philosophy and framework as well as how to think positive, live positive and make positive choices...

What is your destiny?

G: Getting over yourself

O: Overcoming your odds

H: Hesitancy, Heart, Honesty, Hustling and a Healthy balance

A: Anger and Artillery

R: Remembrance, Resilience, Restoration, Renewal and Righteousness

D: Dreams, Depth and Destiny

PART VII

WAYS YOUR PARENTS CAN HELP YOU *"GET OVER IT!"*

I really think that everything that is new is not always better…some things that we learned as kids are relevant in contemporary society. Sometimes we need to remember those positive aspects so we can use them in our struggles for significance and ability to *Get Over It*. And sometimes we have to help others so that they can help us. This may require conversations. Here are a few ideas that you can share with your parents/guardians and discuss about helping you to *Get Over It!*:

1. Let me be a teenager…Let me think like a teenager and act like a teenager.
2. Listen to me. And although I know that it still may not make a difference in your final decision, I think that I need the opportunity to express my feelings.
3. Surround me with positive people who I can depend on. Trust the people that you surround me with …that they will also lead your child in the right direction with the "right" advice."
4. Know that I am a unique individual and should be treated as such. Please recognize and embrace that I have a unique personality and different needs and sometimes my needs have to be addressed individually.
5. Talk to me.. Keep those lines of communication as open as possible. Will I tell you everything? Probably not. Will I tell you something? Hopefully so. But only if you have built that type of relationship with me where I feel you are really listening to what I am saying.

6. Play with me. Not just when I am a baby are and toddler but now…as a teenager. Yes, the games will change but let's do it in an effort to continue building that unique relationship with me that is based upon love.
7. Fight for me. You are the best advocate for me. Now I am not saying that you should embrace wrongful actions that I may have committed but you can still show support when the school requests your presence for the disciplinary conference. While you are there let the administration know that while you don't agree with my actions you will continue working with me to improve my behavior. And if you don't agree with the administration I think you should still try to have a healthy discussion about the situation.
8. Do some creative things with me. I have gifts and talents…Discover and embrace them.
9. Remind me of where I come from. I'm going to share with you a "real" example here…I get on my oldest son Najja's last nerve when we are having a discussion and I tell him "you came from my cootie so therefore…" or I will say "do I have to remind you of the cootie story?" Mind you, Najja is now 22 years old and I will say this wherever we are…the food store, his campus, in front of his friends, etc. I do this as a gentle reminder to him that he belongs to me so I should come first (after God) until he has his own wife and children. Sometimes the exchange is funny but other times it can be a serious situation. He learned how serious I was about me being first during a recent visit home.

Najja came home for a couple of weeks this summer and decided to have a "small" party in honor of his "brother" Nate (the kid who lived with us during high school). Nate was leaving for Afghanistan (where he was deployed) and it was the first time the boys had been home at the same time since high school. We allowed them to have this party that grew to about 75 kids...no loud music or obscene behavior occurred but our neighbors called the police because the kids were "too loud" and since there was a noise ordinance the neighbors felt the kids were breaking the rules.

The police came to our home, inspected the situation and noted that the kids were actually well behaved but cautioned us to keep them inside so their voices wouldn't "carry" so far. They also noted that they believed some of the kids (most of the guests were between the ages of 19-22) had been drinking alcoholic beverages and suggested that my husband and I "check out" each kid before they left to ensure the kids did not attempt to drive while intoxicated. Although we knew that Najja and Nate were not serving alcohol we are "wise" enough to know that some kids may have brought their own. We really didn't have a problem serving as the "sobriety police" until about 4am that morning (for the safety of the kids). As a result of this we did have several kids (male and female) spend the night because they were too tired and they may have had too much drink. Through all of this Najja remained calm, level-headed and very thankful to his parents. He was extremely respectful to the authority figures (the police), used his manners and behaved like the perfect gentleman. He remembered "where he came from." He didn't even fuss when I awakened him after only 2 hours of sleep to go to church service at the 8am the next morning.

Now, fast forward two days later when he invites a few more friends over...Now remember, this story is about reminding your kids where they come from and who should be the most important person in their lives. So Najja has his friends visiting in the basement and we carried on with our normal routines upstairs. I'm not sure what time his guests left that night because they were watching television and playing pool when I went to bed. What I do know is that the next morning when I went to get a glass of orange juice the *entire* container of my Tropicana Pure Premium (no pulp) orange juice was gone. You know, the jug that costs at least $4??? *Gone*!!! My reaction was "WTH?"

I woke Najja up and sent him on his way to the food store to buy more orange juice. He didn't argue because he knew he was wrong on several accords…he came back with the wrong orange juice (I hate pulp) so I sent him back. He came back again with the wrong type (he just bought a bigger jug of the wrong orange juice). By the 3$^{rd.}$ time I sent him back to the store he was clearly agitated and began to tell me that the store "didn't have it" and how the saleslady couldn't find it either. This boy had the nerve to tell me that I was just going to have to settle for that big ass container of orange juice with the pulp in it. What? Are you kidding me? So the juice sat on the counter with the receipt under it for a day.

On the evening before he was to depart back to college I asked him when he was going to return the orange juice and he noted that he had not planned to because I was being ridiculous about it. Ridiculous? Me? Well, that was it for me because I had to remind this 20 year old that he didn't have a "pot to piss in nor a window to throw it out." I reminded him of everything that I had done for him in his lifetime (including serving as the sobriety police two nights before), that I was his mother and he should *want* me to be happy, etc. I told him that the car he was driving at school was *my* car and he was no longer able to drive it. I told him I was coming to Buffalo for it and all the "extras" he had been receiving would no longer happen because he didn't take care of me as I had always taken care of him.

After I carried on for at least twenty minutes he got up, took the jug of orange juice, went back to the store and returned with the *correct* orange juice. Tropicana Pure Premium (no pulp). I guess it was all a bit much for him so he packed his bag quickly, made a few calls and then left the house. He went to a friend's house where he spent the night and the next day he left for Buffalo (where he attends college).

We didn't speak for a couple of weeks until he finally called and said he was sorry. I wasn't convinced that he knew what he was sorry for so I explained to him my hurt and disappointment. I was hurt because I felt as though he forgot where he came from…that he came from a family where we make sacrifices for each other because all we really have in this crazy ass world is each other. I was hurt that he wanted me to "settle" when all of his life I never allowed him to settle nor did I teach him to "settle" for second best or for something he did not want.

I was hurt because I felt he wouldn't "take a bullet" for me, as his mother, and that's what you are supposed to do. I told him that he should have gone to 10 stores in search of the right orange juice for me because I am his mother and he came from me…there is only one of me and that's what you do. I have never shortchanged him and I have four sons so how could he do this to me and he only has one mother. I reminded him of the "cootie" story and this time it had a serious effect on him because he realized or remembered the depth or significance of this. I think he looked at our relationship and expectations of this relationship on a different level because he was a "man" now and responsibility comes along with being a man and having a mother.

Yes, it was a long, drawn out argument over the orange juice but the lesson learned here was a blessing earned. My children know they are loved to "infinity and beyond" but with that love does come sacrifice...I think Najja forgot about that when it came to the orange juice and needed to be reminded of *where* he came from and *who* he came from. So hopefully you won't have to go through all of this drama for your own kids to understand but the importance of remembering where they come from.

10. *Ask for help if you need it to deal with me.* You are not a bad parent if you ask for help. You are simply a parent who needs help...this is where the notion "it takes a village to raise a child" comes in. Sometimes the "best" parents need someone else to step in and assist.

11. *Discipline me.* Now I know that we all have our own philosophy about what the best way to do this is but you have to discipline your kids. I need to know that there are consequences for my actions and that for every action there will be a reaction. I need to know my boundaries and if I cross those boundaries there will be consequences.

12. *Praise me.* I am never too old hear how smart I am, how special I am, how creative I am, how pretty I am, etc., etc., etc. I *never* stop wanting to feel your love and your words of praise is symbolic of that.

Ask your parents to think about how they feel as adults...they say they really don't care what others think but they really do. It still warms their hearts and makes them feel a bit more confident and special when they receive a compliment or praise from someone and they know that it is coming from a good place.

13. *Reward me.* I think this is aligned with praising me. These rewards may not have significant monetary value but my psychological and emotional value extends beyond the

almighty dollar.

14. *Give me a home…not just a house.* I believe that I deserve to have a place where I feel safe, secure and wanted, I should have an address that belongs to me and my family. Even if it is an extended family household I need to know that this is my home and not just somebody else's house that we are "staying" in.

My maternal family described to me a time when my mother and I did not live with my grandmother but I don't remember (I was 5 and younger). I only remember living on St. Marks with Mom Belk and the constant arguing between Ma and my grandmother. The argument usually ended with Mom Belk finally saying "Get out! This is *my* place and you can just leave!" Ma would then tell me to pack a trash bag because we were leaving. I would throw whatever belongings I had into this bag and then sit in the front room on the couch and wait. Our trash bags would be sitting at the door and my mom and I would just sit on the couch. And we would sit some more. It was somewhat eerie to just sit in silence so eventually I would fall asleep and would wake up the next morning and still be in the same spot. It was only when I got older that I realized that we sat because my mom didn't have anywhere to go. So I sat with her – trying to feel her pain and make it disappear but I was lost in my own sea of confusion and doubt. I always tried to understand why we lived the way that we did. Why couldn't we have our own place to live and why couldn't I have my own bed? I didn't have my own bed until I was 14 years old! I knew that this way of life was "deeper" than me and there was never a sense of "peace." I needed to feel as though I had my own home and couldn't be thrown out. Or, that I wouldn't have to pack my things in a trash bag and wait for my next move. A child needs to feel like they have a home…not just a house where they "stay." So, don't worry about the size of the home, the furnishings in the home or the address of the home…what matters is that the child can say "this is *my* home."

15. *Laugh with me.* Sometimes you just should listen to my jokes, watch me dance, hear me sing and enjoy a funny television program with me so you can share the laughter. I've heard that laughter is soothing to the soul but I really think that listening to me laugh strengthens the spirit as well.

16. *Share your feelings with me.* Please let me know how you feel about situations. Now that doesn't mean that you have to share explicit details with me but please allow me to see you experience various emotions…happiness, sadness, a bit of fear, uneasiness, some anger and lots of confidence. I really think that it is healthy to let me know that raw feelings are never "right" or "wrong" but it is what you do with those feelings that make them right or wrong. I need to know that it is okay to cry but I don't have to cry over everything. Sharing feelings with me can only help me to cope with my emotions and it allows me to recognize that there are positive outlets to release feelings.

17. *Mandate "quiet time" for me.* It's synonymous with "me" time. Quiet time is a great springboard for meditation as they get older because they won't be afraid of their own thoughts. I will already know how to be alone with myself and dream about the possibilities. I will already know how to respect peace and tranquility because that's what I strive for during quiet time.

Raising children is definitely a complex task with diverse

methods and fascinating dimensions to the outcome. The good aspects, with the adverse aspects, together, are the creative raw materials of your children's spiritual, academic, social and emotional growth (this was adapted from my line's "greet" as a pledgee). Parenting doesn't come with a manual of instructions for everything nor is there a "parenting for dummies" manual to help you through it. It is different for everyone...I've made mistakes...lots of them but I use the lessons learned from those mistakes as blessings earned so I won't make the same mistake twice.

I didn't know how to be a mother when I became one so I took bits and pieces from the moms that I knew to create my parenting program. I knew what I didn't want to be as a mother by remembering some of things Ma did that had a negative impact on my well-being. I knew I wouldn't teach my kids to lie to cover my butt, I wouldn't hurt them psychologically, emotionally or physically and I knew I would teach them how to love unconditionally and not to fear love. I knew I would always protect my children and they would know that I am always there for them...no need to fear being alone because I would always take the reins and take care of them. These were the things that I think Ma lacked as my mother.

I think about the time I was in a horrific car accident when I was about 13 years old when I had to take a cab home from my mother's friend's (male) house where she had passed out in a drunken stupor. I wanted to go home because it was late on a Sunday night and I wanted to get ready for school the next day so Mr. Mitchell called a cab for me, put me in it and sent me on my way. This was something that we had done on several previous occasions so we didn't think any about it. The difference this time, however, was that another car swerved in front of my taxi and we crashed into a pole. My face hit the bulletproof shield between the driver and the passenger and I sustained injuries to my mouth, teeth and jaw. There was a lot of blood and as a child the police and ambulance immediately rushed me to the emergency room at the hospital.

I remember the police questioning why I was in a cab that time of night and where my mother was. I lied and told them I didn't know and I told them I was coming from my friend Yvonne's house where I had spent the day but they could call my grandmother and she would come and take care of me. I was rushed to the hospital where they called Mom Belk who walked to the hospital and immediately began asking where my mother was. I couldn't tell her because I was sworn to secrecy by Ma and I was too afraid of the consequences if I did say something. Ma didn't protect me from the accident and even though parents cannot be in all places at all times with their children, I think that somebody needs to be able to reach them at any time.

I remember crying hysterically because my face hurt so badly and I was scared of all the blood. The nurse just held me in her arms and kept saying "baby, it's gonna be alright." My mom should have been saying that to me. It should have been my mom hysterical on the other end of the phone, running up to the hospital and bursting through the doors looking for her "baby." Instead, the nurse held me until Mom Belk got there and my grandmother reminded me that although I was alone in the car accident I wasn't alone in life. She said she would be there for me always and reminded me of how much she loved me. I believed her but wished that it was Ma saying those words to me.

I think that somehow I knew at that time that I could never be a mother like that because it just didn't feel right. I loved my mother so much that I lied to protect her when she should have been there protecting me…this is not my idea of who a "good" mother is. My mother never knew I was in that accident until the next day when she arrived home. When she saw me with a swollen face and stitches in my mouth she was a bit confused about what happened to me but immediately wanted to know if I told anyone where she was. She never took me in her arms to console me and tell me that "everything was going to be alright" as the nurse had done in the hospital. Her actions were just wrong on so many levels and I bore the burden and consequences of those actions. I knew from way back then what would *never* happen to my children as long as I was breathing and walked the earth as their mother… I learned this as a 13 year old girl.

I did see other examples of what "good" moms should be doing though and used to pray that my mom would one day show an inkling of what I saw in the others. I knew that there were good qualities in my mom because she had to be the "strongest" black woman that I ever saw at that time. I saw her fight for social issues in our neighborhood and lead a celebration for "Black Solidarity Day" in my elementary school. I saw her start a *LOUD* protest on a city bus when I was eight years old because she didn't like the way the bus driver spoke to the kids boarding the bus. I also saw her publicly speak in Albany, New York to fight for basic necessities for my junior high school. And I also saw her punch Ms. Wilson in the nose after Ms. Wilson made the mistake of waving her finger in Ma's face and threatened to "kick her butt." Yes, I saw a "fighter" in Ma and I know that when she was alive I was a fighter in training under her watch. Her incredible resiliency of spirit is what allowed her to cope for many years with her own inner pain. Despite these positive qualities she was still lacking in other areas as my mother but I have forgiven her because I learned in college about the effect of alcohol on your ability to use sound judgment. I honestly didn't know that she was considered to be an "alcoholic" and didn't know this until I was given her death certificate and it said "cirrhosis of the liver" as the cause of death. My Uncle Marsh had to explain to me what this meant because I really had no clue. But you know what was so weird? I don't think through it all that I ever felt totally unloved by her...I just didn't think that she did a good job of taking care of me as I watched the mothers of my friends take care of them. It sounds odd but I think she has done a better job of taking care of me as my mother in her afterlife than she ever did while on earth.

I used to only pray to God to help me through many crises in my life but on the 30th anniversary of her death I had a wonderful "conversation" with Ma. I explained to her how I felt about many things...You see, although I had forgiven her a long time ago and did not harbor any resentment I never really had "the discussion" with her as an adult child. Once I did that on this death anniversary she explained to me that she was actually there for me, had always been there for me but I had simply not asked *her* for help. She described how she saw me grow up to be this amazing adult despite and in spite of everything that happened to me and around me. I realized that she was correct...I always prayed to God for guidance and never to my mom. I guess I thought that she wasn't really there for me when she was alive so how could I possible count on her in death? Well, I was wrong.

I began by talking to her nightly and then asking her thoughts about things happening in my life. Then I began to pray to her for guidance...often asking "Ma, what should I do?" Amazingly she sent answers to me....Now I know this is challenging to believe but my husband is my witness...I would tell him "I prayed to Ma last night and here is what I asked her for help with..." Within a short period of time many of my issues were addressed. This happened on numerous occasions that a running joke in our house when problems arise is "have you asked Ma for help?" Ma is now my "secret weapon" and I save the best for last when my back is against the wall. I've included her in my arsenal of artillery that I talked about earlier and I'm better and stronger having my mom back in my life in a healthy relationship. Yes, I still pray to my God but praying to Ma comes right along with it.

Ma was negligent in her motherly duties while she was alive and I looked to the mothers of my friends for maternal guidance. My childhood best friend Bertha had a mom that I considered a "fashion diva" because Bertha always had the latest and the greatest styles in clothing. I knew then that when I became a mother my children would be dressed "sharp." Aunt Louise was the mom of my closest high school friends and her warmth, compassion and openness with her daughters inspired me to want that relationship with my own children. And then there was Mrs. Lunden affectionately known as "Ma" on my block...so many of us lived with her for periods of time in our lives...Her house belonged to all of us who needed it and this showed me how the "village" is supposed to work. I knew that between living there when needed and watching how Mom Belk always opened her doors that my own house would be a "home" for those I could help. Taking all these pieces of motherhood helped me to center my own ideology of what it should be and who I should become as someone's mom. I wrapped it all up and became me.

Please know that I am far from a single parent so I can't speak to that experience as an adult. I have a husband who not only loves and adores all of his children, he still loves and adores me. This combination has made our child-rearing easier for us. I'm not sure how I would have handled situations without his support or the support of family and friends in our lives. What I have described to you is only based on what the philosophy that I have used to raise my own children...it is definitely not a "fool-proof" method. I've shared with you how I became the mother I am today and the "rules" that I use to guide me along the way. I know that my children are unique individuals and I accept all of them for who they are...from the core of their souls and this may require varied parenting styles.

Below you will a few "Mama Musts" that I use in my life to help raise my children. These are the basic fundamentals that I use daily to "perfect" my job as a mother. Perhaps your mom uses some of the "musts" on this list too...

"Mama Musts"

1. *Mama must* love her children for who they are and not just for what she wants them to be (do not question who they really are).

2. *Mama must* listen to her children share their dreams and not confuse them with her own (their dreams are the key to *their* futures).

3. *Mama must* demand respect from her children but must also teach them how to earn respect through her own actions (walk the walk).

4. *Mama must* be firm, fair and consistent in her household rules (sets expectations).

5. *Mama must* always follow through on her promises and consequences (demonstrates dependability).

6. *Mama must* wear her tiara around the house periodically to remind the children who the "Queen Bee" is (so that they can remember to treat her as such)

7. *Mama must* allow her children to evolve into the incredible adults that they are destined to be (don't smother their personalities)

8. *Mama must* let her "no mean no" and her "yes mean yes" (children will learn that she doesn't "flip-flop").

9. *Mama must* let her children know what topics/issues are non-negotiable (not everything is up for discussion).

10. *Mama must* be able to act like a mama, but sometimes think/understand like a child (to empathize with their perspective).

11. *Mama must* not be a best friend until the child is an adult child (they have friends their own age for this job).

12. *Mama must* set the standard for her children about how a lady should be treated (never letting herself be mistreated in front her children).

13. *Mama must* teach her children that her love and commitment is given to them from her heart at "no charge" (children need to know that some of the best things in life can be "free").

14. *Mama must* always remind her children that she loves them to "infinity and beyond."

15. *Mama must* simply "be there" for her children but also "be real" with them (this includes the good, the bad and the ugly).

What do you think your "Mama Must" do to help you "Get Over It?"

PART VIII

JUST "PLAIN OL' STUFF" TO *GET OVER IT!*

1. *Be nice to folks.* It's amazing how it's so difficult for some people to just be *plain ol' nice* to others. As though it would be impossible to say something nice even if you really don't care. You just do it because you know it will make the other person feel good. I do this all the time and it makes me feel better knowing that I've made someone else feel better even if it's only for a minute. On the days that I may feel despondent I do this as a bit of a "spirit filler." I can feel like crap and everything around me seems to be going wrong but then I choose someone whom I have contact with on that day and I may say something nice to them ("OMG! I absolutely love that shirt/blouse!!! When I grow up I want to be just like you!") It doesn't matter if it really is the ugliest shirt/blouse known to mankind and I would *never* be caught wearing such an atrocity...the point is that person is now smiling outside and inside because you noticed what they had on and you gave them a sincere compliment from your heart. The teen years can be tough years and we never know what people are going through. Sometimes are kind words can be the best words some people will hear all day.

This fills my spirit and makes me feel more positive in the most negative circumstances. Some folks haven't received a compliment in days, weeks, months and years. You just never know what the impact of saying something nice to someone has on them. I do it frequently, especially when I am feeling miserable because it really does fill my own spirit and makes me feel good about myself knowing that I made someone else feel good...if only for a moment in time. Just be nice. *Plain ol' nice sometimes.*

2. *Get on your knees and pray sometimes! Just plain ol' on your knees* on the side of your bed prayer. Not a quickie "shout-out" before you go to sleep or when things are going from bad to worst in your life. I mean having that true conversation with God or your spiritual motivator. Talking out loud about your feelings, the good, the bad, the confusing, the emotional turmoil, the mistakes, the success, etc. Whatever it may be that is happening in your life…have that discussion and thank God for all opportunities.

   Thank God for your blessings and then pray for more blessings and pray for other people. Pray for your "worst enemies" and for those who just may need Jesus in their lives. But be sure to give God *all* of your attention at that moment while on your knees. I think sometimes we treat prayer as a chore – we do it because it is a part of what we are supposed to do and it needs to be done. Instead, we should embrace the opportunity to fill our souls with the spirit of God…we take that for granted until something goes wrong then we are the first to scream out for Jesus. Make it not only a practice, but a promise. Promise yourself that you will get on those knees without interruption and give God your undivided attention. I do it…not daily but I know I do it enough that when I stand up I stand stronger, wiser and definitely fulfilled. Just get on your knees and pray. *Just plain ol' prayer.*

3. *Learn how to say "I'm sorry" and mean it. Just plain ol' "I'm sorry."* I've met so many folks throughout my lifetime who have the most difficult time admitting they were wrong *and* saying they are sorry. I struggle with why folks do this because saying sorry doesn't mean you are a sorry person. It simply means that you are sorry for what happened. It doesn't mean that you are less than who you really are *or* that you are more than who you really are. For me it is not an ego trip or a power

struggle; it simply is a sorry. Isn't that what we teach our children? If they do something wrong (intentional or not) to someone else then the quickest way to resolve any conflict is to embrace your behavior and say "I'm sorry?" Think about it...most of us were raised that way...to apologize.

We were also taught as children that we cannot control whether the apology is accepted but if we have done something wrong we need to apologize. So why do so many folks struggle with this concept as adults? Is it because the perceived stakes are higher emotionally, psychologically and perhaps financially? For me, I think allowing myself to admit a mistake helps in my humility because it reminds me that I am not omnipotent. It is a gentle reminder that although I am very intelligent I don't know everything and actually there isn't a need to know everything, so if I do something in error it's because there is learning in progress.

I've learned to embrace when I've done something wrong I should admit that it was wrong, say that I am sorry, try to make it right and then I need to "keep it moving." No wallowing in self-pity and no making excuses for my behavior. While pledging my sorority many years ago we had to memorize a saying "Excuses are the tools of incompetence which build monuments of nothingness. Those who excel in excuses seldom amount to much at all." Simply stated, own your mistakes and recognize that there is nothing right about being wrong and there is nothing sorry about saying you're sorry. Learn how to say "I'm sorry" and mean it. *Just plain ol' sorry.*

4. *Learn how to just "walk away." Just plain ol' walk away.*

You don't have to fight and argue about *everything!* When my oldest son attended Montessori school in the early 1990's and I would visit the classroom I noticed that the teachers often told the children to "walk away." At first I was a bit puzzled then I understood that the children were learning to just walk away from potential conflict or bad choices. It was a simple statement that required discipline to do. Sometimes we struggle when we have to walk away because at times we think if we walk away then we are walking away without our pride intact or that we are "giving up" or "giving in."

Walking away doesn't have to mean this and I have discovered that it requires making choices and finding that healthy balance, that "gauge" that I wrote about earlier. Frankly, some arguments with some people are just not worth my time or my energy. I always "consider the source" before deciding to walk away…I ask myself "who are you and what type of person are you?" I mean, why should I let you jack my day up because you are determined to be "right" and want to antagonize me? Go ahead and be "right" in your own little world and I will take the rest of the day being "happy" because I was able to walk away.

Know how to walk away from the things and people in life that deposit negative energy in your world. Those are what I consider to be the "quickie" walk-aways (like the secretary who gets on your last nerve, the colleague who always has something negative to say, the brother or sister who constantly is "starting" with you). Professionally you can always say that you "turned the situation/person over to Jesus" and personally you can just tell them to "kiss my ass!" Whatever the situation is you must always be armed with the choice to simply "walk away."

There are emotional relationships that are bit more complicated to just walk away and sometimes this is soooo hard because we want to do the best thing and the most appropriate thing but will question if it was the "right" thing to walk away. My husband and I have recently experienced this. His mom lived with us for eleven years but the last three years felt unbearable to us for a myriad of reasons. Yes, she is elderly and sickly but she can also be a very miserable lady with a negative disposition. We decided that we needed to find her a safe and secure place to live after experiencing a significant amount of emotional turmoil due to her behavior.

We made that choice to "walk away" from the negative facet of this relationship so we could get back to positive vibes in our home. His sister finally found a personal care home for her and now we have lifted that burden. Yes, it was challenging and it did not happen in a day but the bottom line is that you first have to choose to release those toxins and just walk away. *Just plain ol' walk away.*

5. *Have some manners. Just plain ol' manners.* Somewhere in this digital age we have reduced the usage of manners. What happened to "please, thank you, excuse me, I beg your pardon, etc.?" I think we still learn this as children but we seem to accept a life without them as adults. I take great pride in using my manners and showing respect...even to those that I question are deserving of it. This is instilled in my children as well...they have learned early on that when I call them they are not allowed to say "Hunh?" and "What?" because I think that reeks of rudeness. And as bad as this may sound, I would rather have an *ugly* child than a *rude* child. My children are not only respectful with their manners with adults they are required to display their manners with their siblings and their friends. I demand this behavior so that it will become second nature to them as they mature into adults. They won't have to think about it when their supervisor calls them...they won't respond "Hunh?" or "What?" because they would have been conditioned to respond appropriately.

Manners make a difference in how you are treated and how you allow yourself to be treated. Folks do remember how you treat them as well and I believe that good manners are an example of respect. Even if you have done something wrong and you still remember your manners I think that you can have a positive impact on someone. An example of this happened when my son was a sophomore in college. Apparently he (or his roommates) had been charged with dorm damage and were supposed to complete community service as a consequence. This should have been completed prior to them being allowed to register for courses the following semester. Of course *my* son did not complete his community service and his registration was blocked.

As the "helicopter mom" that I am, I called the housing office to get clarity on exactly what needed to be done to remove the hold on his account. Well, the gentleman that I spoke with said "I have to admit that although your son was flat out wrong, he had to be the most well-mannered 19 year student that I ever met." He continued by saying that Najja was clearly frustrated and disappointed that he couldn't get the hold lifted but he still remained respectful to the workers in the housing office. The director actually said it was "amazing" how well-mannered Najja was and he thanked me for raising such a polite son.

Najja still had to complete his community service but we were able to get the hold temporarily lifted to register and then they immediately placed it back on his account to prevent any other type of activity. I believe that it was partly based upon Najja's manners and my respectful approach to the situation. Soooo, remember your manners because they can make a difference when you least expect it. *Have some manners, just plain ol' manners.*

6. *Begin to forgive folks. Just plain ol' forgiveness.* This may be

extremely difficult to do when you feel as though you have given all that you can and people seem to hurt you anyway. Or, if you are an innocent bystander and you are still hurt. How do you or how can you forgive the people who have inflicted pain on you or in your life? It's hard y'all. It is hard but we have to do it to move forward. This is something that I initially struggled with as a young girl but then I realized that if I spend so much energy harboring negative feelings and holding on to "old" hurt then I would be chipping away at my positive energy that allows me to love. Once I forgive someone then I can move forward and they no longer take up space in my life. God knows how many times I have been hurt in my lifetime...it feels as though I was born into a maternal family who prides itself on not forgiving one another. Holding on to situations that impregnated them with heartache and pain and protecting that hurt with anger and negativity.

My uncle died a couple of years ago and I think that he died with lots of unresolved conflict and bottled up anguish. Uncle Cleve never forgave me, and never forgave my mother. I was never forgiven for an argument that we had when I was 14 years old on the night of my mother's wake (3 days after she died). I tried many times over the years to mend fences with him and I apologized profusely on several occasions but his response was still the same "You and your mother..." You see, Uncle Cleve and my mother (according to the family) *never* got along as children, teens and adults. Actually my Uncle Marsh and Aunt Caren (my mom's siblings) told me that my mother was just "mean" to Uncle Cleve and used to make fun of him...they never got along and I believe that he never forgave her for that and as *her* child he couldn't find it in his heart to forgive me.

On the night of my mother's wake I kept talking about missing my dad and I couldn't wait to see him. Finally Uncle Cleve exploded and began to berate my father. I was shocked at his reaction, appalled at his response and basically argued that he was wrong. I told him that I had just lost my mother and how could he have the nerve to try to take my father away from me! I was a hurt and confused teenager and I did lash out but I was so sorry about it afterwards and kept telling him this for at least 15 years. I consistently tried to reach out to him by calling him and visiting him but he never forgave me for my words uttered (well, I was actually screaming) on July 18, 1980. He died in July 29, 2010. While alive, Uncle Cleve missed 30 years of my life and only met my oldest son as a young child. He never embraced that I was *not* like my mother in so many regards and that I was a successful woman with great promise and a positive life because he never forgave me. I think about how he missed out what a loving, responsible, diligent, tenacious niece (the only one he had) I am and all that I had become. He missed it because he could not forgive me.

Now I know all of this goes deeper but it is an example of how the inability to forgive can destroy relationships. I forgave Uncle Cleve many years ago for his insensitivity, selfishness and unyielding ways and when I flew to New York for his funeral in 2010 I arrived with a clear conscious and apologized to him *for my mother*. I told him I was sorry for what my mother had done to him as children, teens and into adulthood. I also told him that I hoped he would be able to finally forgive her since they would now be in the afterlife together and could create a new relationship. I reminded him that I was only my mother's child but I was *not* my mother and I was sorry that we never were able to have a relationship since I was 14 years old. I touched his hand as he lay in the coffin, I told him that I forgave him for not loving me the way I needed him to but it was alright and I was okay because I had forgiven him a long time ago. After that I stood up, made my sign of the cross as a Catholic and walked away.

Walking that uncomfortable road of forgiveness is not easy but I think that it is necessary and required to be a "true" Christian. It is the "heart" of what it means to be Christian. This includes forgiving yourself which is sometimes the hardest thing to do. We can't figure out how to forgive ourselves so we turn to God and pray for forgiveness. We often think that if God can forgive us, then that will empower us to forgive ourselves. It is imperative that you learn to forgive yourself or you won't know how to forgive others.

Forgiving oneself allows oneself to love unconditionally and have the confidence to let negativity go. We often stumble over this. Letting go of "stuff" is a key component in forgiving…I've known many people in my lifetime who forgive but never "forget." I really believe that it's not truly forgiveness if you cannot forget. If you keep bringing up the same ol' stuff and acting the same ol' way then you haven't released it all and you have not truly forgiven. Should you let the person who hurt you travel in the same lane with you again? I'm not sure about that because you don't want to be stupid about it. You certainly can forgive and choose not to have that person in your life anymore or change the way they are in your life but harboring negative feelings is not reflective of forgiveness. It goes back to that old saying "What would Jesus do? Ask yourself "How many times has God forgiven me?" Hmmmm…*Begin to forgive folks. Just plain ol' forgiveness.*

7. *Keep your mouth shut and stop tellin' folks your business. Just plain ol' keep your mouth shut.* I know I can talk too damn much sometimes and tell a little too much. I have learned over the years though that I can't tell all of my business because folks search for failure and will use what you say against you…even if you shared it with them in confidence. They often have their own issues (such as jealousy) and

will have great pleasure in sharing your secrets. If you are married, keep married business in the marriage. If you have children, teach them that family business is just that...family business. And, if you have good friends then don't go around telling their business. This is all linked to honesty and trust and you have to maintain that in your relationships for them to remain positive.

You can help yourself by really picking and choosing what you will share, how you will share it, and who you will share it with. A question that I always ask myself now is "Would **** want me to share this information?" I think of the person or persons who may be affected by my words and that helps me to decide. For example, I *know* that my ol' man doesn't like me to talk about him on Facebook so when I do plan to mention him I "feel it out" with him first to gauge his reaction. If he doesn't seem to embrace the idea then I leave it alone. Even if I feel it's my business to tell also...it's just not worth the hassle and argument that could ensue because I shared his business with the world on Facebook. If we have a disagreement I don't always vent with "my girls" because that ain't their business either. There are times, however, that I may be hurt or confused, will seek advice from a friend and will have to share some of my marital concerns but it is still done in a respectful way.

You have to be *real* careful with whom you share your story with. Not everyone just wants to read your words...many want to retell the story in their own way for their own benefit. So, sometimes you just have to keep your mouth shut and stop tellin' folks your business. *Just plain ol' keep your mouth shut.*

8. *Stop doing stupid stuff. Just plain ol' stop doing stupid stuff.* No long explanation here. Y'all know what I am talking about...the same ol' dumb stuff that we all do. The stuff we keep doing the same way but expect different results each time. Never cleaning up our own dirty

dishes...putting those plates in the sink again and again and expecting someone else to clean them. Well most of the time that doesn't happen so it's stupid of us to do it...but yet we still do. We do those same all stupid things and expect different results. For me it encircles finances. I keep doing the same ol' stupid stuff with my money because I just don't respect it as I should. I've put my credit cards in envelopes and put them in the freezer, I have created accounts with small limits, I've "saved" in retirement accounts and countless other methods to let my money work for me but at the end of the day I still do the same ol' stupid stuff with it. I know better but I don't do better and it's a lesson that I am still learning. Get a grip on the stupid stuff that you are doing and start the process of stopping it. We are all stupid at some point in our lives...embrace your stupidity, learn from it, grow from it and keep it moving. You can begin to do this by creating your "stupid stuff" list and begin to create a plan of action to eliminate the items off the list...Take it one stupidity at a time so the rate of recidivism is low. Once you create this list you'll really see how stupid you really are after-all (lol). *Stop doing stupid stuff...just plain ol' stop doing stupid stuff.*

9. *Don't forget to wipe. Just plain ol' don't forget to wipe.* Yep, I said it! If you forget to wipe then you will actually stink and everyone you come in contact with will smell you. I am using this metaphorically because sometimes we forget to look deep within ourselves and embrace our flaws. We tend to walk around and pretend that our "stuff doesn't stink" and feel as though we are better than others. We need to wipe away these negative attitudes and pretentious behaviors.

I remember growing up in the "ghetto" in Brooklyn and going to other "ghettos" and thinking that every other ghetto was worse than my own. That's ironic to me now because a "ghetto is a ghetto" but I used to think that when I went to the Brownsville, Red

Hook or East New York sections in Brooklyn or to the projects that I was actually "better" than those folks there. I felt that since I lived in a brownstone apartment (without heat, hot water and with the roaches and mice) that somehow my physical dwelling was better than the projects because "those people" were on welfare and my family was not. Since where I lived was "better" than I was "better." I would go to these areas and walk around as though my stuff didn't stink but a rude awakening happened to me when I was attacked by Clarence in his house in East New York, Brooklyn. It was there that I learned that it doesn't matter who you are and where you live *anything* can *still* happen to you. Where you lived was really not who you were. If my physical dwelling actually reflected who I was then what did that make me? I grew up in economic poverty but did that make me intellectually, psychologically and spiritually impoverished?

When you come across some folks and some situations your background, money, education, familial ties, employment, etc., just don't matter so you shouldn't lean on those shields for perceived protection. You have to just "be you" and hope that it is enough. This requires that you wipe the negative thoughts and feelings of superiority away. You need to be "squeaky clean" as you travel down these roads called "life." Don't pretend that your shit doesn't stink and don't forget to wipe away those negative attitudes and pretentious behaviors. *Just plain ol' don't forget to wipe.*

10. *Get stuff that fits. Just plain ol' get stuff that fits.* How many times are we disappointed when we find that "perfect" outfit and the store doesn't have it in our size? And ladies, how many pairs of shoes are in your closet that you *knew* weren't exactly your size but you bought them anyway because they were cute and you felt you could "make them work?" Well, you can always regroup and find another "perfect" outfit and you never have to wear those shoes again if they hurt too much,

but you can't do that with your life. Do things that fit your lifestyle and the significant people in your life.

I never borrowed worries by taking my tribe of children to upscale restaurants or the adult theatre because I knew that I didn't have children who could "sit." My boys were "all boy" and would wiggle around, get under the table, on the floor, climb all over me, etc. Yes, I did have control over them (for those of you saying "why couldn't she control them?") but their personalities dictated that they needed to explore their surroundings and for my baby Zuri, he needed to sit on me wherever we went (he suffers from separation anxiety). My take on this was to select places we could go that were family oriented where I could teach the kids how to behave in an appropriate manner without it being a penal atmosphere. My kids learned their "restaurant" behaviors at places like the Golden Corral and Fridays.

When Najja was in high school we would take the entire family at least once a week to the Golden Corral for dinner and they would say their grace, get their plates and walk with me or my husband up to the buffet to select their food. They learned how to stand in line without pushing, not take more than they could eat, not touch everything, watch their surroundings, not run in public places and they were able to practice their manners with the servers. It was a great fit for the Johnson Tribe and I am grateful that I did not expose them to places where they did not "fit." If I did this then I couldn't just take the experience back like a pair of shoes…it would be a permanent part of their lives. Instead, I chose and I still do choose places where my children and I can feel safe, secure and comfortable. *So, get stuff that fits. Just plain ol' get stuff that fits.*

11. *Walk on the "wild side" now and then…Just the plain ol' wild side.*
Sometimes you have to take chances and walk on the "wild

side" to know what really makes you happy. As that "square" that I shared with you earlier I tend to stay within my box and I really don't take too well to changes because of the fear of the unknown. But I also know (and I've been told) that I have a "wild side" that only a few people are privileged to witness. No, I don't have a secret life as a stripper/pole dancer, do undercover drugs nor am I a closet alcoholic but when I feel safe and secure I tend to relax a bit more and this could be considered my "wild side."

I really think that we need an air of excitement within our lives...just simple enjoyment. As we age we also begin to take life so seriously because our responsibilities are serious and there really isn't a lot of time to just enjoy ourselves, soak up the sun and think of nothingness. Everything we do has to have a purpose or we won't include it in our calendar of events. Now I'm not saying you should get out there and get stupid...but you should just get out there periodically to see that the world still exists and it doesn't necessarily revolve around you. You can't just say "stop the world, I want to get off" because you really don't control the world but you are a part of it. Tap into your "wild side" and embrace it as a part of you so you can enjoy it when given the opportunity and you won't feel guilty once you are enjoying yourself. We all have a little "crazy" in us and sometimes we have to embrace that craziness to maintain our sanity. Do something that you didn't like to do before and do things that you absolutely love. Stop taking every moment of every day so seriously and let the good times roll. *Walk a bit on the wild side...just the plain ol' wild side.*

12. *Take pride in yourself. Just plain ol' pride.* I think that you should always remember that your name is always attached to your

actions, words and work. Knowing this forces you to give everything that you have when doing something. Knowing that you are worthy and the trail you leave behind you should reflect this as well. At the end of the day it's your name that is attached to it all.

I know that I come from royalty…not economically or politically but from generations of "Belks" and "Whites" who take great pride in their heritage. Two sides of my lineage that represents themselves as kings and queens in the family despite economic impoverishment. My family demands that we are treated well because we treat ourselves well and we give our best in accomplishing goals. We take pride in our products and work hard to achieve   As Jean Belk-White and P. Anthony White's daughter I know that my brains come before my beauty and that pride comes before the final product so I *Get Over It!* and I don't allow myself to hit the actual rock bottom with this pride. Some folks may interpret my self-confidence as arrogance but I think that's just because they truly don't understand the imaginary tiara I wear everyday outdoors that reflects my royal pride. See, I already know that with pride comes dignity and with dignity comes respect. I often say that it doesn't matter too much if someone likes me or not… I just demand respect. I demand it because I give it and I demonstrate that I am worthy to receive it. Having pride is a part of the total picture of who I really am and how I *Get Over It!*

Mom Belk taught me to be a lady. Ma taught me stand tall and stand up for myself. Daddy told me to remember to "be smart and be cute and everything else will follow." These are the lessons that are positioned at the base of my pride and instilled in my daily actions and these are the things that allow me to continue to *Get Over It!*…despite and in spite of life's circumstances and folks around me.

Take pride in yourself. Just plain ol' pride.

13. *Going ol' skool sometimes. Just the plain ol' skool.* Sometimes the lessons we learned as children can serve as powerful motivation as adults. There are things that I was taught as a young girl that I still hold on to and embrace as an adult that are extremely helpful to my daily existence. I learned that when you say "please and thank you" it makes a difference in the approach that others have toward you. My mom used to require us to look in her eyes when she spoke to us "Look at me when I am talking to you" so now having direct eye contact is never a problem for me. I learned how to "pay it forward" before the term was coined because Mom Belk always showed me how to give to others because God has blessed me with so many things…I had no idea what those things were at the time but I learned how to make my Kool-Aid sweeter without adding more sugar. And then I learned how to share that same Kool-Aid with someone who may have needed it more. Going ol' skool doesn't mean bringing old baggage with you…it simply means using the knowledge you learned as you were growing up to make you better and stronger…Think about some of those things…What are you doing today as a result of what you learned yesterday? *Going ol' skool…just plain ol' going ol' skool.*

PART IX

Twelve Tricks to *Get Over It!*

1. *When something is itching, scratch it. If you don't, it will keep itching.*
   Don't ignore the things that cause you pain. If you do it will continue hurting even if you mask the pain.

2. *Don't just buy things just because they "look good."*
   Make sure they are good for you. Remember that everything that looks good on the surface doesn't necessarily look good in *your* life. Always imagine *yourself* and *your* life in a situation before you just jump into it because it "looks good."

3. *Just because you can't sing doesn't mean that you should only hum.*
   You may not be the next Rihanna, Beyonce or Chris Brown but never deny yourself the opportunity to enjoy things! You can enjoy doing something without having an ulterior motive.

4. *Remember that a bucket can be filled one drop at a time so you don't have to fill it in one shot.*
   You can reach your own ladder of success by climbing one rung at a time…you don't have to race to the top just to get there. And remember that the small things eventually build up to the bigger things in life.

5. *Dreams don't come with a warranty or a guarantee.*
   It's your job to ensure that they are never broken.

6. *One man's junk may be another man's treasure but you don't have to accept it.*
   Never accept anything secondhand unless you want to because you are not a secondhand person. But if you decide you want to accept it then make sure it is worthy of *you*…

7. *Know the difference between courage and courageous.*
   We are all born with courage but it's when we use it at the right time that makes us "courageous."

8. *Spiritual, emotional and mental paralysis can have a worst impact than physical paralysis.*
   If you don't feel anything in your heart, your soul and you don't use your brain then you have paralyzed your ability to live a worthwhile life. At least with physical paralysis you can still live a fulfilling life…I'm not convinced that you can do so if you are living with spiritual, emotional and mental paralysis.

9. *You own the power of change.* So change it.

10. *Life isn't fair.* But so what? What are you going to do about it?

11. *Bringing volume to your silenced voice doesn't mean you have to shout!*
    Instead, it means you may have to adjust the sound on someone else's speakers.

12. *Don't leave without your bag.* Make sure that after the end of every relationship you fill your bag with knowledge and lessons so that you can grow from the experience. Your bag should be filled with what you need to learn and grow from the relationship…the good, the bad and the ugly.

PART X

WHAT YOU NEED TO *GET OVER IT!*

You always need to be conscientious about your strengths and your weaknesses (SWOT analysis). Create a list so you can work on it daily. Here is a sample of the things that I am still working on:

1. *Learning how to say "no."* I suck. Simply put. I try to be all things to all people all of the time and I have difficulty saying "no" to be a part of things, to do things and to make things happen for others. I want to be at the forefront of change and be that change agent in the lives of many. As a result I become overburdened with responsibilities and each day can become a 25 hour day so I can make things happen. If I would just say "no" to some of these things it would allow more flexibility in my life. I'm at a point in my life when I don't have to be "Superwoman" so I don't need to be involved in everything…Just say no.

2. *Learning to say "no" AND not feeling guilty about it.* I suck. Simply put. This is one of the main reasons that I don't say "no." I can't deal with the guilt that I feel that I actually let someone down and didn't help them. Perhaps it is just my nature but I feel that as long as I can help folks then I should. If I don't help then I feel guilty about it. This can be tied into learning how to "walk away" a bit more. I need to be able to walk away not only from conflicting situations but from situations that can survive without my interference and intervention. Sometimes the best help we can offer is to just stay out of it…I need to learn how to be comfortable with saying "no," staying out of it and not feeling guilty about it.

3. *Balancing my need to control.* I suck. Simply put. This is challenging for me because this can also be one of those things that is my greatest strength and my greatest weakness. Because I always

have visions of how things should be and need to be I work to make it happen. I spend countless hours *going hard* to ensure quality but sometimes I need to let go a little more and just "Let God." Yes, I believe that my God has all of the answers but sometimes I don't immediately see the answer so I try to control the outcome. While this is a good characteristic to have in the general scheme of life I want to learn how to lean on my shield of faith just a little more so I can give total control to my God.

4. *Accepting defeat.* Now that's a hard one for me to swallow…When you have spent your entire life fighting for everything that you have…your sanity, your love, your family, your children, your marriage, your education and your economic stability it is near impossible to accept defeat. I don't even think I know how to do this. Yes, I know how to walk away when I am ready but to walk away because I "lost" is a foreign notion to me. I *Get Over* so much in my life that I immediately look for different angles to approach situations. As previously noted I look at many rules as starting points toward change. I know that I don't have to fight for everything and that I make sure that I pick and choose my battles. But to be defeated in one of those important battles? NOT!!! I absolutely have to work on this…Hmmmm…do I really though?

5. *Learning to live with Lupus better.* I know that generally I cope with my disease well…I never let it stop me from doing whatever it is that I want or need to do. But that's not always the right approach. When I'm sick I just need to let myself be sick and do what it takes to get better. I have to do a better job of stopping and taking care of myself despite of "who needs what." Just taking my medication daily is simply not enough when you are living with Lupus…it's a disease that requires more attention mentally and physically because each day is different. I can literally wake up today and feel perfectly fine but

tomorrow I may struggle with just getting out of the bed. That's when I just need to stay in the bed and learn to listen to what my body is telling me. Yes, I need to learn to live with my Lupus better so that I can do better, be better and *bounce back* better.

6. *Letting people love me*. I still have some of those walls surrounding my heart and that's why I have that invisible square around my life. Sometimes people just want to love me because I am lovable and I ask too many questions about their intentions. I think this is linked to my fear of loving too many and loving too hard because then I will have to *lose hard* if something happened. I think that we need to let others (positive people) who want to love us have the opportunity to love us. Sometimes that's all folks want to do...love us.

I also think that I spend too much time trying to figure out *how* they want to love me. Throughout my life there have really been great people who loved me the best way that they knew how but sometimes I rejected that love because it didn't fit my schema of how I should be loved.

I really do need to let more folks beyond my family love me. I'm not sure where it began but I have never been a gracious "gift-receiver." I've always thought if someone was trying to give me something then they must want something in return. I felt it was a way for them to buy my love and believed that any fool knew that you can't simply buy love. What I'm still working on is the fact that sometimes people already love you and they want to give you a gift as an expression of that love. I need to learn to accept that this is all that it is...it is what it is and I need to let others love me.

I just wanna love you baby...

He only wanted to love me.

And I wouldn't let him.

He only wanted to take my heart.

And I wouldn't give it to him.

He only wanted to share my soul.

And I wouldn't show him.

I wouldn't because I couldn't.

The emptiness inside of me ran so deep

That plugging the hole with love really didn't seem to be an option.

So I didn't let him love me.

I didn't open myself to his love.

And I didn't allow myself to feel his love.

I didn't allow it because I couldn't.

But he kept on wanting me to love him

And he kept showing me how to love

And he never stopped loving me

And he never stopped believing that I could love him back.

He believed in love and worked at making a believer of me.

But I never loved him back.

I didn't because I couldn't.

And so he kept on loving me.

And I kept not letting him love me.

And then he stopped.

He said he couldn't love me anymore.

Because I didn't love him back.

And then he went and loved someone else.

Because she could love him back.

I "coulda, woulda, shoulda" but I didn't.

Because I couldn't.

CONCLUSION

This is my story…only mine and it is not research based…only reality based. This book has been about aspects of my life and what has worked for me. I don't claim that there haven't been many mistakes and stumbles along the way but I have shared with you things that have worked…the positive things that have allowed me to live in peace daily and not borrow worries. I've been a teenager before and I get how difficult it can be. I know that the world around you doesn't always hear what you are saying, feel your pain and see your greatness. But I also know that everything happens for a reason and that you go through things to move forward. I've had lots of negative things happen to me in my life but these experiences have only made me stronger, wiser and more in tune with my sanity.

I've learned to *Get Over It!* through tragedy and triumph and I've learned to *Go Hard* through efforts. Some of my life experiences I would never wish upon my worst enemy because I don't think that anyone should have to go through pain and suffrage to understand how to live healthy lives and be happy. I don't want my kids to be like me in this regard because no one should know pain as I have in order to live a quality life. I want to teach them tenacity without torture, courage with compassion, persistence without pressure and humility without harassment. They can be strong without excess inner pain and they can be soldiers without having to emerge from those trenches of hell. I think that you can too.

I've shared those experiences that I believe had the greatest influence on my life but there are countless others that I am simply just not ready to talk about. I could share stories about daily living with Lupus, my eight years of infertility, my complex but poignant relationship with my dad, betrayal, and other physical violations in my life, issues with men, etc. Things about me that I have never disclosed to anyone because "anyone" just doesn't need to know…at least I think they don't. There are many other stories about triumph, trepidation and tenacity…stories about my life that can make you laugh, cry and just shake your head. I am so proud of myself in many regards and but am truly embarrassed about some choices that I have made in my life. There is just soooo much more to my story that sometimes I think my life belonged to someone else and it couldn't possibly be me that I am writing about. The pain is still raw in some instances but for other experiences I've let the emotion go and would have to "re-live" the emotional experience to write about it in depth. I don't want to be that "provocative victim" and solely focus on my stumbles. Perhaps time will allow me to address those experiences in another written format but for now, I just wanted to answer that question "How do you do it all?" I just wanted to explain what it means to *Get Over It!*…I wanted to describe the process it took to get to this point…to the "finished me" (well, I'm not finished yet but you can see how far I have come) and I wanted to really express how your approach to your life makes the difference in the quality of your life. I still question the difference between "luck" and "blessed" but I treat each day as a different gift in life. I un-wrap each gift every morning with the same excitement and exuberance as the day before. My life is a gift from God and I face each day energized over the possibilities.

I know that some people interpret my self-confidence as arrogance but that doesn't stop me from wearing my tiara around the house while dressed only in shorts and a t-shirt. You see, I know that I come from intellectual and spiritual royalty and I know I deserve to be treated like the queen. If I'm the queen then my boys know that they are 4 princes and that's another positive lesson to teach them! When I look in the mirror at myself with my tiara on this serves as a gentle reminder to me that I am made of the same good stuff that "official" royals are made of so I deserve the "best" in my life. I have to continue to *Get Over It!* to have the "best" and I have to always look on the positive side of things to be the "best." When I pledged my sorority I was given the name "Positivity" and that's how I approach each day…positively.

There has been no formal policy or practice but instead a plethora of ideas that shape my daily existence. I've had lots of support from my family…maternal and paternal, my friends and just from folks who love me. My Uncle Marsh, Aunt Caren and Aunt Cecilia have been those much needed surrogate parents over the years. And my paternal cousins have always "had my back" and supported me through it all. Although their lives have been different from mine but they have always, always, always been there for me. Although not biological, my sorority sisters have been amazing to me over the years…Janessa was there with me as I delivered Najja, Nichelle is my better financial half and always has her couch and shoulder ready for me when needed. LaKeisha has always supported me in any way that I needed…I could go on and on but my sorority sisters, particularly from the Gamma Iota Chapter in Buffalo, have always given me the family security I needed when I had to *Get Over It!* Individually or as a group, they have been my "rocks" that I have leaned on over many years. I think it's important to have that "go-to" person that you know will always be there for you and actually listen to what you are saying. I've maintained the same group of friends from high school and college who also serve as a support system for me.

Who is your "go-to" person or persons? Know who they are and use them! Choose a "usable and touchable" role model that you can learn from based upon your reality. Find that person that you emulate and dream about following in their footsteps. Don't base your selection of this role model on material things, such as the type of car they may drive or the zip code where they live. Don't choose this role model by determining how "cute" they are or who their life partner may be either! And, I'm not just talking about an entertainer that you admire, I'm talking about a real, live person that you have access to, can talk to, and ask questions and who cares about you and your dreams. These are the type of people you need in your support system. Fill your network with role models who want to teach you and see you live a healthy and prosperous life.

The first person who I defined as my "real" role model lived across the street from me on St. Marks and I was determined to follow along the same path that she trod. She didn't even know that she was my role model until I was an adult and we reconnected. It was because of Sheryl that I was introduced to the world of Alpha Kappa Alpha Sorority Inc. and the collegiate experience. Fast forward many years later and I still stand in awe of her strength, intellect, beauty and tenacity and I yearn to be like her as I continue to mature. Yes, you absolutely have to find that role model who is a part of your daily life and incorporate them into your support system. You definitely need that to *Get Over It!*

Getting over yourself, Overcoming your own odds, Heart, Hesitancy, Healthy balance, Honesty, Artillery, Anger, Remembering, Resilience, Renewal, Righteousness, Dreams, Depth and Destiny serve as the foundation to *Get Over I!* in my life. They have been the core of my being and have helped me in this lifelong struggle for significance and quest for knowledge. To help you to focus on the above I have created a list of questions that you should ask yourself. I think that by honestly answering the questions will force you to recognize who you really are and perhaps why you really are this person. This is definitely an essential component to *Get Over It!*

1. What are your likes?
2. What are your dislikes?
3. What are your strengths?

4. What are your weaknesses?
5. What are your fears?
6. What are you proud of in life?
7. What things bring you the most joy?
8. Who or what would you "take a bullet for?"
9. What are your dreams *now*?
10. Who is your role model?
11. What are some of the things that you still need to *Get Over it!* about?
12. What are some of the things that anger you?
13. What are your strategies for dealing with that anger?
14. What are some of the things that you need to "let go" of?
15. What are your blessings in life?

Through my academic preparation I've learned that there are basically ways of knowing…6 ways to know what we know about life --- tradition, personal experience, intuition, logic, expert opinion, and research. This book has focused on the first four because they have been the cornerstone of my existence and have made a difference in the choices that I've made throughout my life. I still maintain certain traditions in my life such as getting on my knees to pray as my grandmother taught me and using my personal experience to remind me of how to honestly complete my SWOTs analysis. I also follow my intuition because it is directly linked to the way I think and how I feel. And finally, I cannot defy logic so I must use deductive and inductive reasoning to help me in the decisions I make. Remember, I explained that I think through most decisions and I use logic to reach my final choice. These four ways of knowing have always been a part of my *Get Over It!*, get through it and keep it moving approach to life because it provides explanations about "why I do what I do."

Although you've never sat in my chair at the same time, danced in my stilettos to the same beat or tossed in the same bed as me in the night I do think that you can learn from my experiences and use my suggestions as tools to move toward positive change. But, keep in mind that since you've never bathed in my bath water you can't really pass judgment on how to best cleanse my soul. I am still a work in progress and I still dream about my future. I still have wants and work daily to reduce my needs. I still hurt over the loss of my mother at such a young age and in many ways I still feel guilty over her death because I couldn't do more for her. I know that I am an enabler but I'm still not sure if I want to stop being this type of person. I still wish my brother and I could have a loving, "normal" relationship. I wish that I lived with my dad for longer periods in my life as a child because it could have made a difference in my experiences. I have always loved and respected my dad so much that I wish he was a daily part of my life growing up. And I wish that I weren't so mentally "needy" but I can't spend my days borrowing those worries. I have to simply keep living and *Getting Over It*.

I'm not sure who put it there...

Sometimes I feel as if I'm just in a state of being

And all I do is exist

Like I keep climbing this mountain and I never seem to reach the top

And it all seems to hurt

But you can't take away the pain because I'm not sure who put it there. I feel like I move quickly from "A" to "Z"

And I never stop in between

But all I know is that it hurts

Sometimes I feel as I'm being punished –

As if I am Eve eating the forbidden apple

I just don't feel real

And I blindly combat my daily enemies

And I know it hurts

Because I can feel it

But what can I do to make it right? To make me feel real?

But you can't take away the pain because I'm not sure who put it there.

Sometimes I feel those tears rolling down my cheeks

But I'm not sure what they are for

Are they remnants of my pain? Or, are they tears of joy?

How does it all fit together?

Is what I seek really out there for me to find?

All I know is that it hurts

And you can't take away the pain

Because I'm not sure who put it there.

<u>My Mask</u>

I think that it is at the times when I am really understood

That you can feel me cry.

It is then my heart is on my shoulder

And I walk with a limp.

It is now when my brown eyes become shady and hazy

And my smile doesn't show my real feelings

It is at these times when you will really know me, that you will feel my pain through the laughter and the games.

It is now that you can hear my thoughts as they grow and see my brain begin to expand

And notice that my mask has changed, that I need your outstretched hand.

I think that it is at these times when I really need you,

That I believe I fail you,

That I don't know you,

That I can't feel you.

It is at this time when you must search through my tears, remove my mask and love me anyway.

It is at these times when I love you the most…but can't really say.

I feel so afraid and like I'm no good

Could you love me anyway?

I am hesitant and frightened of what may be,

Can you hear what I'm saying, do you understand me?

It is at this time that you should feel my pressure and ask to support me more

Perhaps deliver me from my own evil, remind me of all that's good and what my purpose in life is for.

Yes, it is sorta, kinda what I ask of you…to know me when I need you to but not sure I want you there.

But you hold my hand anyway to help erase the fear.

You take away that mask because I won't need it with you

And reaffirm my significance, all the good that I do.

It is at this time when I need you the most that you will be there for me

And it is then that I'm okay with living without my mask…to live naturally.

My life shows that I have always been on a mission to push through the pain and to move towards positive change…My exterior is definitely tough…hard…but my insides, oh my, they are still so soft…so vulnerable. I still struggle for significance despite and in spite of many obstacles. I just get over it, I get through it and I keep it moving. I don't borrow worries, I just don't have the time to. I'm a busy woman with a full agenda and I don't need the additional weight to slow me down. I've got things to do and people depending on me to do them…My great-aunt Naomi taught me that I may be "weak in my body but I'm strong in the Lord" so I know that God orders my steps and that I am His servant and not man's. I also know that I walk in His path and not the road that many have tried to lure me down that is created out of pebbles and stones. Some days my road may be the road less travelled but then there will be fewer lanes to cross and fewer negative folks to deal with.

I have to *Get Over It! to Go Hard and* to live right…That's the only way I know how to live. The only way I know to move beyond hurtful places. I *Get Over It! and Go Hard* so I don't have to *Hurt Hard* and I have been successful because of this drive. I know now that you must first change the way you think before you can change the way you behave. I think that you have it within yourself to make changes as well.

A few years ago one of my supervisors said that she was tired of hearing that people should "pull themselves up by their bootstraps to be successful." Her concern was "what if folks don't have any bootstraps at all to pull themselves up from?" She was making the point that some people have nothing and therefore can't see a better tomorrow because they are stuck in yesterdays and barely functioning today. I don't agree with her thoughts and I don't think you should either. I think that *not* having bootstraps is actually impossible as long as you have faith. I don't think that my God has put anyone here on this earth without the ability to have faith in His creations. For some it is more challenging and they may hear more "no's" than "yes's" in their lives but I think that if you hold on to your bootstrap of faith then you know that "your time" is coming. Everyone's story is different but we all need to thrive on the faith that has been God-given and use this faith as a bootstrap to pull yourself out of any pits of despair, disappointment and disenfranchisement. The stories that I have shared have been examples of how I used my own bootstraps to pull me up, how I used those same bootstraps to bring volume to my silenced voice and how I hung on to those bootstraps when I stumbled on many occasions. I've used those same bootstraps again and again to bounce back after hitting rock bottom.

Life as a teenager was rough for me...it wasn't always a "happy" time but it was the time for me to live, learn and grow. I had dreams and worked to make those dreams come true. You can do it too! Find your bootstraps and dust them off! Hang on to your faith and you will also move toward positive change in your own life.

So that's it...that's all I have for this book. It may be a bit much for some of you and others will say "That ain't nuthin' compared to what I've been through..." But the key point is for you to understand that despite and in spite of where you have come from, what you have been through and if you have hit "rock bottom," you can still bounce back and rise up to fulfill your dreams. Recognizing that your life is going to be alright if you believe in yourself, your dreams and what you are capable of doing. Your past does not have to determine your future but your today will definitely affect your tomorrow. What will you do today to make a difference tomorrow? It all starts with believing that you can "Go Hard" and knowing that you are okay with that. For me, I embraced the concept "I am, I can, I will, I do" so I have... So yes, this is my story but it's only that...MY story and how *I* do it. This is how I *"Go Hard so I can Get Over It!"*

"I already know that I am "so much," but what's even better is that I know that I am destined to be "so much more!"

INSPIRATIONAL THOUGHTS TO HELP YOU *GET OVER IT!*

Polar Opposites

Without fear there is no courage.
Without sadness there is no joy.
Without pain there is no pleasure.
Without hate there is no love.
Without conflict there is no peace.
Without enemies there are no friends.
Without struggle there is no significance.
Without sin there is no forgiveness.
Without inequity there is no justice.
Without mental enslavement there is no intellectual empowerment.
Without weakness there is no strength.
Without loss, there is no gain.
Without questions there are no answers.
Without negative signs there are no positive signs.
Without death there is no life.
Without choices there are no decisions.
And without hope there are no dreams.

Lesson: Life is full of experiences, emotions and "things" that are two sides of the same coin. The two "go together, fit together and heighten each other. Each contributing to the ultimate bliss." Sometimes you face the "worst" in your life before the "better" emerges along your path. But know that it is coming because your life is abundant with polar opposites and you are competent and blessed to own the power in order to balance your own scales...Weigh yourself carefully.

Get Out!

If someone is hurting you then why do you want them in your life?
If someone is abusing you then why would you need them in your life?
If someone is consistently lying to you then what is the purpose of them in your life?
Hmmmm....

These are questions that you have to answer from deep within yourself.
You have to dig deep, face the truth and deal with the issues within yourself that allow you to accept these people in your life.

I don't think that we intentionally place a "welcome mat" at the front door of our lives to invite negativity in. But some of us become that "provocative victim" where we play games and start things that we have no intention of finishing and we build relationships that we knew were unhealthy from the start and then we wonder "what happened?"

We see the signs way ahead that direct us to make the right turn out of the relationship but yet we still drive straight ahead into the abusive and negative situation because we are searching for a love/relationship that may never exist with this person.

Or, we keep trying to "change" that family member because we think they are supposed to love us in a certain way just because "we are family." And then we are the ones hurt. We feel betrayed. We feel lost. And we feel confused.

You see, most relationships make you feel that way sometimes anyway but it's when it becomes consistently unhealthy that we must learn to just walk away. We must learn that when it's time to go...It's just time to go. Whether it's the relationships we have with our significant others, family, friends or bosses. If it hurts us worse than it soothes us then we have to question why we really need it in our lives.

Sometimes people love us the best the way they know how and then we try to change that love and train that love in order to breed a new love. But that just doesn't work either. We can't control how people love us...just how we accept that love. You own the power of change so you can change who you let love you... And if it hurts real badly, just let it go. Take yourself through the mourning and healing process of letting them go out of your life.... Love them differently now...Or don't love them at all. Love yourself more and know when you've had enough. Yes, hurt hurts...That's what it is supposed to do. But letting go releases "stuff" and that's what it is supposed to do...

So let go of the hurt, lies, and emotional, psychological and/or physical abuse that may encircle a relationship that you are in. Let go of that negative relationship you may have with your own self because sometimes we hurt ourselves more than anyone else is capable of... I could go on and on but it's simple...Know when it is time to "walk away." And know when it is time to "Let go and Let God."

Lesson: Examine the relationships in your life and own that power of change to determine which relationship you need to walk away from.

More or Less?

Sometimes "more" is actually "less." The more you have, the less you want or need.

Let me explain:

You see, the more you have of God in your life is the less time you have to deal with the devil. The more faith you fill your spirit with is the less self-doubt that you feel daily.
The more love that is in your heart is the less hatred that flows through your bloodstream.
The more dreams you have leads to less nightmares of what your future will be.
The more clarity you have on your goals is the less confusion you'll have about your purpose in life.
The more positives you attract in your world is the less negative energy that will gravitate towards you.
And the more you keep open, honest, inspiring people around you, the less "drama" will come into your life.
The more self-empowered you become is the less likely you are to give up on yourself.
The more goals you achieve are the less failure on your list.
The more you give is the less you have and the less you probably need anyway.
The more you become that man/woman of your word then the less folks will question your integrity.
The more you love yourself, the less you will depend on others loving you the wrong way.
The more self-esteem you build, the less opportunity others

have to tear you down.

Oh yeah, the more cute you believe you are inside and out then the less ugly you will allow others to make you feel.

The more you allow yourself to trust and believe in the steps that God has ordered for you is the less you'll have to ask about the path that he has chosen for you to follow.

You see, we are already "so much" but we are destined to be "so much more."

And that's okay if it uplifts and strengthens your life...

More faith, more positivity, more love, more confidence, more assurance, more empowerment...

Ah yes, "more" of the right stuff is "less" of the wrong crap... More is less.

Lesson: Fill your life with "more" of the things that will empower you... It's the only way to guarantee that your weaknesses will be "less."

Loving on Me...

There's something about loving yourself that makes you feel whole.

There's something about trusting yourself that makes you feel honest.

There's something about believing in yourself that makes you feel that dreams can come true. And there's something about thanking God for creating you just as you are that makes you feel special.

So why do always forget these things?

See sometimes we don't embrace how beautiful we are, how smart we are and we focus on the things we are not.

We don't think about all the good we have done but can quickly write a list of all the wrong we've a part of.

And we don't remember that we are important and we deserve more because we have trained ourselves to settle for less.

Why is it so hard for us to be good to ourselves?

We wrap our hearts around other people first and then we try to love ourselves with whatever is left.

But that's not enough.

Our souls need more to give more.

Our spirits require more to share more.

And our emotional well-being thrives on positivity to become more.

But if we always neglect who we are to focus on what we think we should be then how do we appreciate the person who we live with today?

I know we all strive to accomplish things in our lives but sometimes we just need to be *STILL*. We need to listen to the voices within.

And feel the strength of our inner selves... We can love ourselves stronger this way.

And know that we really are independent, free-spirited, priceless and honest...Enough to love ourselves to "infinity and beyond."

When was the last time that you looked in the mirror and said "I Love You!"?

Hmmmm....

But yet we tell others every day.

And we show them in so many ways.

You see if we don't love ourselves, affirm ourselves and commit to ourselves then how do we empower ourselves?

If we don't pay more attention to ourselves and to who we really are then at some point when we look into that mirror again we will be staring at an empty reflection...at a person

that never really was.
Yeah, there's just something about lovin' yourself that makes you stronger...And makes you happy to be you so much longer...

Lesson: Don't forget to love on yourself first...You have to love you, trust you, believe in you and empower you before you are any good to anyone else.

The Bottom Line

The bottom line is that you are responsible for your own dreams...
You cannot expect anyone else to make your dreams a reality for you.
You have to create your dream and work your dream to live your dream...That's your responsibility so don't expect others to do it for you.

The one thing that I have learned throughout my life experience is that the more you depend on others will be the more that you will learn to depend on yourself because folks just won't get it done for you.
But why should they? Is it their dream? Is it their investment? Folks can support you to infinity and beyond with their love and positive thoughts but don't wait on them to do things for you...
They mean well but they have their own dreams to fulfill so you can't expect them to work on yours.
Sad, but it is ultimately true.
You are the only one who can make your dreams become a reality for you so begin to create your plan of action.

When developing your path to your destiny you should include those things that are "perfect" so you can always see what you are trying to achieve but also include the "worst possible scenario" so that you are well aware of what could go wrong.

Know that the path you take could be the road less travelled but that's okay because that only means that there is more room for you to navigate on the road to greatness.

Know that your path may be full of pebbles and rocks but those are only the stepping stones you have to climb to achieve your dream.

And know that it may not be "easy" but it is "easiest" if you remain positive and grounded.
There may hear a lot of words such as be "No, Maybe and I'll See" before you finally hear that "Yes" but that's just a part of the movement...

Be prepared for the work...get your mind right and know that this is what you really want to do because at the end of the day it is your dream that you are following and you are responsible for it.

Some folks may interpret your confidence as self-arrogance and others will view you as a "pillar of strength" as you struggle for your significance in your dream.
Be prepared for that as well but know that you are on a mission to work that dream to live that dream...despite and in spite of others.

It's okay to question yourself, check yourself and change yourself along the way but never lose sight of who you really are…

You may have to "play some games" to get where you want/need to be but know that these are just games you are playing and remember who you really are under it all…

So, I've said this before but it is appropriate again…
What happens to a dream deferred?
Nothing. Absolutely nothing.
Don't let it happen.
Period.

Your dreams are your responsibility…they don't belong to anyone else so don't give them away…
Nurture and nurse those dreams as though you gave physical birth to them…
Treat them as though they are your children…
Most folks do not give their children up for adoption so don't give your dreams away either.
Love them.
Respect them and work for them so that they ultimately remain positive dreams and not scary nightmares…

Ah yes, those dreams are real and the responsibility is really yours…
Take the responsibility and make it a reality.

Lesson: The Dream is Real. Work it to Live it.

ABOUT THE AUTHOR

Dr. White-johnson is the author of *"Go Hard and Stumble Softly"* published in July, 2012. She is also the author of *"Get Over It! How to Bounce Back after Hitting Rock Bottom"* and *"How to Get Over It! in 30 Days."* In addition, she has created a leadership and personal development program for teens that is aligned with the national Common Core Standards and the American School Counselor Association National Model Standards. She earned her Ph.D. from the University at Buffalo and holds a master's degree in the counseling field. Dr. White-johnson is married and the mother of five children.

[ii] http://nces.ed.gov/programs/digest/d10/tables, Institute of Education Sciences, National Center for Educational Statistics

[ii] http://en.wikipedia.org/wiki/SWOT_analysis

[ii] http://en.wikipedia.org/wiki/Dreamcatcher

Made in the USA
Charleston, SC
17 November 2013